CLASSIC CUISINE OF
PROVENCE

Pour Huguette … Niçoise d'origine; Niçoise de coeur

CLASSIC CUISINE OF
PROVENCE

DIANE HOLUIGUE

Illustrated by *Skye Rogers*

TEN SPEED PRESS
Berkeley, California

CLASSIC CUISINE OF PROVENCE

Text copyright © 1993 Diane Holuigue
Illustrations copyright © 1993 Skye Rogers

1👁

TEN SPEED PRESS
P.O. Box 7123
Berkeley, CA 94707

First published in Australia in 1993 by
Simon & Schuster Australia
20 Barcoo Street, East Roseville NSW 2069

A Paramount Communications Company
Sydney New York London Toronto Tokyo Singapore

Text design by Helen Semmler
Additional design work by Michelle Havenstein
Typeset in Australia by Asset Typesetting Pty Ltd

Library of Congress Cataloging-in-Publication Data

Holuigue, Diane.
    Classic cuisine of Provence/Diane Holuigue.
       p. cm.
    Includes index.
    ISBN 0-89815-562-2
    1. Cookery. French — Provençal style. 2. Provence (France) —
Social life and customs. I. Title.
    TX719.2.P75H65 1993
    641.5944'9—dc20   93-19599
                                                         CIP

FIRST PRINTING 1993
Produced by Mandarin Offset
Printed and bound in China

1 2 3 4 5 — 97 96 95 94 93

CONTENTS

INTRODUCTION

THERE ARE MANY provinces in France...but only one Provence. Known to the Northerners as the 'Midi' — the place where the sun sits high in the midday sky — this sun-bleached province with the chalky hills and stony terrain is home to the low slung white or terracotta coloured houses known as *mas* and to the heady 'Mistral', wild wind from the tunnel-shaped valley of the Rhône that whips down the mountains gathering hot, dry air. This friendly, laughing land is where life is lived outside and people socialise at a table with family and friends, in the local cafes, or around the village square where men gather under the shade of the plane trees to revel in the local game of bowls known as *pétanque*, sipping their liquorice-flavoured pastis, talking with a rolling 'r' and pronouncing the last syllables of words with an accent like no other in all of France. This is Provence.

Provence...Provincia Romana. The name came from the Romans, who in 125 BC came first to aid the embattled Phocæans (Greeks from Asia Minor) who had held the thriving seaport of Marseilles since 600 BC, then stayed to make of the region the 'Province par excellence' it was to become. From here, the Romans pushed their domination through all of Gaul, and from this, the period of Provence's greatest history, remnants of magnificent Roman public buildings still stand — the three-tiered stone aqueduct whose aerial bridge, the *Pont du Gard*, spans the cliffsides and reaches down in arched splendour to the river Gardon below; the extraordinary Roman arenas of Nîmes and Arles; Roman baths, temples and a theatre at Arles; a forum, shops and houses of several different styles at Vaison, ruins of fortified towns at Glanum; and vestiges of aqueducts that once reticulated life-giving water to the sun-baked hillsides, which still lace through the Camargue.

After the fall of the Roman Empire in 476 AD, the region underwent a turbulent period of continual attack from neighbouring Visigoths and Franks and from the marauding Saracens. In the eleventh century began an era of relative stability under the rule of the Holy Roman Empire, whose looser control allowed for the rise of fiercely independent regional counties. Most ratified the reunion of Provence with France in 1486, but some sustained an Italian influence for a very long period. Most notable were the Comtat Venaissin, attached to the Papal State, and the Comté de Nice, which was for 400 years linked to Naples through the House of Savoie, and to Liguria and the Italian coast, for whom it was a gateway. Nice did not become a part of the French state until 1860.

To further isolate its cultural differences from the French provinces above it, Provence looks south, its blood warmed by the sun. From the apex of a triangle at Montélimar in the Valley of the Rhône, Provence stretches to the Italian border, where it joins with Liguria, and to the west the triangle passes through the historic towns of Toulon and Marseilles — both modern, industrial towns, the latter the second city of France — to Aigues-Mortes, the fortified medieval seaport of the Camargue from whence Louis IX, Saint Louis, led his ill-fated crusades to the Middle East.

In the centre of the region, bordering the Rhône, lies Avignon, City of the Popes. In the gold-tinged stone buildings of the Papal Palace, popes and antipopes ruled the Catholic world throughout the fourteenth century, ensconced behind the town's towering ramparts. Less elegant, but more lively, is Aix-en-Provence, the intellectual capital of Provence. The hub of social activity is the beautiful plane tree-lined central boulevard, the Cours Mirabeau, where the university students make this one of the most animated and best-loved towns of the south. Its summer music festival brings visitors from all over the world. To the east is the international gateway of Nice, fifth city of France, founded in 350 BC by the Greeks of Marseilles. Now a thriving commercial centre and university town, it is the focal point of the holiday-maker's Riviera.

But if there is only one Provence, there are many aspects of Provence…a Provence of the Alps, with lofty alpine scenery rivalling that of its border countries Switzerland and Italy … a Provence Maritime, that jewel of the glitterati, where the names of the places — Antibes, St Tropez, Cannes, Juan-les-Pins — are as famous as the starlets that frequent them. Here the cliff-hanging, romantic cobble-stone villages call the holiday-maker as compellingly as the magnificent Mediterranean sea, whose turquoise waters give the coastline its pleasure-kingdom name, *la Côte d'Azur*. There is a Provence of the Hillsides, a sparsely populated, undercultivated land, father to the image of the stubborn, hard-working southerner pushing a living against the odds. This is also the Provence of beautiful walled medieval villages, picturesque but unyielding, which climb up rockfaces and perch on hillsides — encampments of the old whose young have moved to town and more recently the retirement idyll of an international clientele. There is a Provence of the valleys and the plains, enriched by the lushness of the river Rhône, and truly the only benevolent countryside on which to grow produce in Provence…and there is a Provence of the Marshlands, the remarkable Camargue, a unique Provençal style Wild West to rival that of the United States of America's.

Then there is the countryside — the countryside of Petrarch's poetry and, later, of Mistral, the first poet to write in the Provençal language and glorify the parched, glaring *maquis* (scrubland) of his youth — where wild thyme and savory course the hillsides, offering little for anything but scattered sheep and a few wild rabbits. Here, too, is the stark, daunting reality of the unyielding countryside of Marcel Pagnol, whose hero Jean de Florette toiled vainly to breathe life without water into his rocky land. There are the bleak mountain passes of Giono's Alpes, so isolated that until the advent of the motor car and the penchant for travel that came with the 1920s and '30s, villages had contact only through sinuous pathways linking them to other communities — more often their alpine Italian neighbours than their fellow French in the valleys below. Then there are the bright, happy colours of Van Gogh's sunflowers, and his little painted bridge near Arles, the colours of Cézanne, born at Aix-en-Provence in 1839, Renoir at Cagnes sur Mer, and the vibrant, strident brushstrokes of Picasso, who made his home in Valauris, and spent months at a time painting luminous blue skies and contented doves.

And for the table…there are the sheep that feed on these savoury pastures, the products of the hunt brought home to be hung and skinned or plucked and treasured for the Sunday meal, there is the olive from innumerable trees, and the golden oil it offers in which to cook. There are truffles from Vaucluse, fruit and vegetables from the garden, or from the lush valley silt-lands of the Rhône, and the Mediterranean to call upon for fish.

There is garlic, anchovies, tomatoes, mountain ham and cheese from the goat and the sheep. There is thyme, rosemary, fennel and other wild herbs, eggplant (aubergine), zucchini (courgette) and wonderful rock fish. The cooking of Provence and the Mediterranean region is one of the most recognisable cooking styles of all France, and when asked to come up with a list of Provençal ingredients, few would get them wrong.

As for the dishes…there is the powerful garlic Aioli, Ratatouille, the wondrous Bouillabaisse, and Salade Niçoise that come easily to mind. Less easily the sardines, and the *tian* of lamb, and perhaps only to the initiated, the deep-fried zucchini (courgette) flowers, the loup (sea-bass) in fennel, the various styles of ravioli, or the *Pissaladière*, French cousin to the Italian pizza.

The Mediterranean diet is one of the healthiest in the world, and the Provençal version one of the most flavoursome. Let's delve in and see…

APPETISERS

HOW BEST TO typify Provence on a plate? Put down an olive — no some olives, for there must be a few black, a few green. Add two or three slices of roasted peeled capsicum (sweet pepper), some red, some golden yellow, a little pile of garlic-flavoured ragout of marinated eggplant (aubergine), and beside this a small piece of stockfish (salt cod), or a few slices of *saucisson d'Arles*, or perhaps some paper-thin slices of air-dried mountain ham?

Imagine a slice of *banon*, the quintessential Provence cheese, made from goat's milk and wrapped for maturation in chestnut leaves, or a piquant *picodon*, and surround one or the other with *mesclun* (mixed salad leaves). Drizzle this with extra virgin olive oil and a dash of red wine vinegar, and again, we'd have the very essence of Provence on a plate.

But then there are frog's legs and snails, *champignons à la grecque*, tomatoes topped with mashed tuna, chopped shallots and olive oil (*à l'Antiboise*), a *salade niçoise*, a wedge of *pissaladière*, a plate of zucchini (courgette) flower fritters…and so on.

There's something fascinating about appetisers. They seem to be indicative of the style of cooking of a region…the hors d'oeuvre is, more than any other course, the essence of a region on a plate.

In the Marché de Forville in Cannes one day, I counted the olive merchant's wares and found no less than thirty-six varieties of olive for sale. There were green olives labelled *Picholines*, others, green and pointed, called *Lugnes*. There were *Grassoise*, *Kalamata,* and the tiny black *Nyons*, often known outside the region simply as the typical 'Niçoise' olives, there were *Nyons sèches* (dried), and *Nyons* matured with herbs, with anchovies or chillies. There were large *Violettes* from Tunisia, green *Sevillanes* from Spain, and *Mamouthes*, enormous black wonders from goodness knows where. There were *olives du pays pimentées* (piquant), or *aux herbes* (flavoured with herbs), some with a *goût anchois* (anchovy flavoured), a *goût amer* (bitter) or a *goût poivré* (peppered). They were pitted, smashed, 'tender', *panachées* (mixed), they were marinated in the *façon grecque*, they were *mixtes et aux herbes*, they were marinated in garlic, with celery, with capers or with garlic and orange peel.

The Provençaux are lovers of olives, lovers of garlic, lovers of vegetables, lovers of olive oil, garlic mayonnaises, chilli, the sun…and life. Any one of the following appetisers will start your meal with that vibrancy and sense of colour and fun of this, the sunniest province of France. For every one is the soul of Provence on a plate.

BLACK OLIVES WITH SAGE

Olives Noires Sautées au Piment

*500 g (1 lb) black olives, preferably
   Kalamata*
*45-60 mL (3-4 tablespoons) olive
   oil*
7 sage leaves
2 small bay leaves
*1 tablespoon coarse-grained sea or
   rock salt*
2 red chillies

Serves 10-12 with aperitifs

THE OLIVE-GROWING AREA of the south of France is legendary. Of the many species available, the tiny black Niçoise olive is the most celebrated, but this recipe is best made with the large, Kalamata-style olive, which is also grown in the region. This warmed olive dish is delicious served with the apéritif.

Drain the olives to remove the brine in which they were bought. Rinse well and dry.

   In a frying pan, heat the olive oil to warm only, then fry the olives about 3–4 minutes, slowly, stirring until they heat through. Add the sage and bay leaves (the bay may be broken up if too large), then the salt, and lastly the chillies. If in doubt as to whether the chilli is too hot for your friends, use large strips so they can remove it; otherwise shred it. Serve warm.

MARINATED BLACK OLIVES

Olives Noires Marinées

1 kg (2 lb) black olives, preferably the fleshier type
1 L (4 cups) olive oil
4 cloves garlic, halved
2 bay leaves, fresh if possible
1 sprig rosemary
2 sprigs thyme
10-15 black peppercorns
3 strips orange peel

Serves 20 with aperitifs

COMMERCIALLY BOUGHT OLIVES are all very well, but to give them your own flavour is infinitely better. Garlic and herbs come to mind readily, but the flavour orange peel gives to the olives here is uniquely Provençal.

Drain the olives to remove the brine in which they were bought. Pack into sterilised preserving jars. Cover with olive oil and disperse the herbs and flavourings here and there throughout the jars. Seal the lids tightly and from time to time stand the jars upside down overnight. Allow the flavours to infuse for a minimum of 1 month before serving. The olives may be stored for months without deterioration.

CRUDITES WITH AIOLI, TAPENADE, OR ANCHOIADE

Crudités aux Aioli, Tapénade, Anchoiade

THE VEGETABLES
Dwarf (baby) carrots
Witlof (Belgian endive) leaves
Small, very white, whole cultivated
    button mushrooms
Cauliflower florets
Tiny radishes
Celery sticks
Thin wedges of capsicum (sweet
    pepper)
Cherry tomatoes

THE DIPS
1 recipe Aioli, Tapénade *or*
    Anchoiade *sauce (see pages*
    140–142)

Serves 6–8

CRUDITES ARE THE RAW vegetables that are arranged on large platters and served as an appetiser in all the regions of France's sunny south. In many areas, the common way of eating these vegetables is with a vinaigrette or a *rémoulade* (mayonnaise with chopped herbs). In Provence, however, the typical mayonnaise would be laced with garlic, made with olive oil and known as aioli. Provence's other favourite dips, both anchovy-based, are the *Anchoiade* and *Tapénade*. Crudités may come to the table with any of these sauces . . . the choice is yours.

Wash, peel and trim the vegetables; separate the leaves of the witlof (Belgian endive). Arrange on a platter as attractively as possible, leaving in the centre a space for a bowl of your chosen dip — the Aioli, *Tapénade* or *Anchoiade* sauce.

The sauces may all be made in advance, but the vegetables may look dried-out if prepared too early. If they do lose freshness, misting with a water spray just before serving may help.

See also *Le Grand Aioli* (page 16), the banquet variation of vegetables served with aioli sauce, and one of the most typical, special-occasion menus of this region of France.

BAGNA CAUDA

Bagna Cauda

THE RAW VEGETABLES
3-4 stalks celery, divided into
batons of about 10 cm (4 in)
1 small cauliflower, in florets
6 small artichokes
12 green onions or baby leeks
24 radishes
2 large red capsicums (sweet
peppers), cut into wedges
24 cherry tomatoes
Leaves of 3 witlof (Belgian endives)

THE PRE-COOKED VEGETABLES
12-18 small potatoes, peeled and
cooked until tender
12 baby beets, cooked until tender
then peeled and trimmed

THE SAUCE
200 g (6½ oz) salt-packed
anchovies — try to buy the dried,
whole ones and remove heads
and bones by slitting or pulling
them open with the fingers, then
chop as finely as possible
150 g cloves (2½ heads) garlic,
peeled and thinly sliced
200 mL (1 scant cup) olive oil
Pepper

Serves 8-10

LITERALLY MEANING 'HOT BATH', *Bagna Cauda*
combines crudités with an anchovy-based sauce,
but differs in that the sauce is served hot and the
surrounding raw and cooked vegetables cold. The
sauce serves to heat, if not cook, the vegetables
and make them more palatable. The end result is
delicious.

Usually a one-course dish, served like a fondue,
Bagna Cauda may be served in smaller portions as
an appetiser.

The vegetables: Trim, cut or otherwise prepare all the
raw vegetables; cut the potatoes and beets. Set aside,
attractively arranged on large platters.

The sauce: Place a fondue pot or similar saucepan
with a burner under it on the stove, and add the
anchovies, garlic and olive oil. Stir with a wooden
spatula so that the anchovies are reduced totally to
a purée — this means simmering slowly just under
the boil, so that they do not crisp, and the garlic
should remain translucent, never browning. Season
with pepper, but no salt. When ready, transfer the
fondue pot to the burner on the centre of your
serving table. Each person takes a turn to dip their
chosen vegetable into the sauce, which warms the
vegetable, and provides a delicious taste sensation.

GRAND AIOLI

Le Grand Aioli

THE VEGETABLE STOCK
1.5 L (6 cups) water
1 carrot
1 leek
1 onion studded with 2 cloves
2 cloves garlic
Bouquet garni: 2 sprigs thyme,
*   1 bay leaf, 6 sprigs parsley*
1 stalk celery
1 stalk dried fennel

THE MEAT, FISH AND VEGETABLES
250 g (½ lb) chickpeas (garbanzo
*   beans)*
15 small potatoes, preferably a waxy,
*   yellow-fleshed variety, unpeeled*
600 g (1¼ lb) small zucchini
*   (courgettes)*
600 g (1¼ lb) small green
*   stringless beans*
750 g (1½ lb) carrots
1 large cauliflower
1 bunch green onions
2 medium beets or 8–10 baby beets
12 small artichokes
*1 kg (2 lb) salt cod (*morue, bacala
or bacalao*), soaked in water for*
*   at least 24, preferably 48, hours*
(see Brandade de Morue, *page*
68)
1 whole chicken weighing 1.6 kg
*   (3¼ lb) or 5 chicken breasts*
36 snails
6–8 hard-boiled eggs

AIOLI IS BOTH a sauce and a dish. At its simplest, it is a garlic-laden dip (see page 140) served with crudités as an appetiser and many people outside France believe this combination to be the only aioli. In Provence, however, an invitation to share aioli most often refers to *Le Grand Aioli*, the traditional one-course meal of salt cod and snails served hot (or warm, but never cold) with a variety of vegetables. The dish celebrates the wonderful harvest of spring or summer vegetables that the Provençaux so prize — their beloved baby beans, artichokes, zucchini (courgettes) and baby carrots. Added to these are the best of the remaining winter crop — cauliflower, beets and chickpeas (garbanzo beans). All are dipped in the golden garlic and olive oil sauce that is so much a part of the cuisine of the south of France.

One of the great rustic meals of all France, *Le Grand Aioli* is best made in spring or early summer when the baby vegetables are in their prime.

The vegetable stock: Put all the stock ingredients in a large saucepan and cover with water. Bring slowly to the boil; cook for 30 minutes, then leave to cool. Strain and return to the pot. This will be used to cook the chicken and warm the snails and, at the last minute, to reheat everything needing to be served warm.

The meat, fish and vegetables: Soak the chickpeas overnight. Cook each of the vegetables in boiling, salted water until tender. The beets and the artichokes must be cooked separately, as both colour the water. Drain the salt cod from its rinsing water, place in cold, unsalted water, bring to just under the boil and simmer for about 8–10 minutes, depending on the thickness of your slices. Cook the chicken

THE SAUCE
*1 recipe Aioli (see page 140) using
8–10 cloves garlic, 3 egg yolks
and 750 mL (3 cups) olive oil*

Serves 8–10

or chicken breasts in the strained vegetable stock until tender (about 45 minutes for the whole bird; 8–10 minutes for the breasts). Drain the snails from their brine, rinse well, and heat in the stock for the last 3–4 minutes.

To serve: Use large platters to serve and arrange attractively with a display of all the vegetables surrounding the salt cod, chicken and snails. Peel the hard-boiled eggs and halve them lengthways, then place on the platters with the other ingredients. Although it is possible to serve some of the ingredients cold, the great aiolis present everything hot (except the hard-boiled eggs) and cooked as near as possible to the time of arrival of the guests to show off the freshness and beauty of nature's bounty at her best.

The aioli sauce itself is the central attraction and, to enhance its importance, is most often brought to the table in the large mortar and pestle in which it is traditionally made. There is no order to this dish — the diners simply help themselves from the platters, and put large spoonfuls of aioli onto their plates.

BAKED TOMATOES VINAIGRETTE

Tomates au Four à la Vinaigrette

6 medium tomatoes, very red
   and ripe
100 mL (½ cup) olive oil
30 g (2 tablespoons) sugar
Sea salt flakes
Cracked black pepper
Few sprigs fresh thyme leaves
9 baby onions or shallots,
   blanched, then halved
Olive oil
Vinegar
Fresh thyme or basil leaves

Serves 6

DELICIOUS IN SUMMER when tomatoes are at their
very best.

Remove the stalk end of the tomatoes and blanch the
tomatoes in boiling salted water. Remove quickly and
peel, cut in half horizontally and squeeze out the
seeds.
   Pour a little olive oil into a baking dish, place the
tomatoes in, cut side up, and sprinkle with sugar, salt
and pepper, and the thyme leaves. Roast at 220°C
(425°F, Gas 7) for 10 minutes. Turn over, place the
halved baby onions or shallots on top, and roast for
another 10 minutes.
   Remove and place, cut side down, on serving
plates. Sprinkle with oil and vinegar to taste, and
fresh thyme or shredded basil.

Variation: Scatter a few hot, cooked, small,
stringless, green beans around each plate as you
serve.

MUSHROOMS GREEK STYLE

Champignons à la Grecque

60 mL (4 tablespoons) olive oil
2 shallots, finely chopped
200 mL (1 scant cup) beef stock
150 mL (²⁄₃ cup) dry white wine
Juice of ½ lemon
3 cloves garlic, finely chopped
15 mL (1 tablespoon) tomato paste
10 g (2 teaspoons) coriander seed,
    crushed lightly in the bowl
    of a spoon
Bouquet garni: 1 sprig thyme,
    1 bay leaf, 6 sprigs parsley
500 g (1 lb) tiny white cultivated
    button mushrooms, stems
    trimmed
Salt
Pepper
Chopped parsley

Serves 6–8 as part of an hors
    d'oeuvre

THE MUSHROOMS ARE not Greek, so perhaps this dish takes its name from the origins of the recipe. Since time immemorial this wine-and-oil-enriched mushroom dish has been a favourite all around the Mediterranean.

Heat the oil in a frying pan and fry the shallots until softened. Add the beef stock, white wine, lemon juice, garlic, tomato paste, coriander seed and bouquet garni. Bring to the boil, reduce heat and simmer for 10 minutes until the flavours blend. Add the washed and drained mushrooms and cook for a further 5 minutes. Using a slotted spoon, transfer the mushrooms to a serving bowl.

Reduce the sauce by one-third to concentrate the flavour. Season to taste with salt and pepper; discard the bouquet garni. Add the chopped parsley and spoon the sauce over the mushrooms. Serve cold, either as an appetiser on its own, or as part of an hors d'oeuvre.

Variations: The Provençal housewife makes this dish with a variety of other vegetables, notably fresh fennel (anise) (thick slices cut lengthways), leeks (whole, small), and even chokos (chayote), or small cauliflower florets work well. Lengthen the cooking time as necessary to ensure the vegetables are tender.

TERRINE OF PROVENCAL VEGETABLES

Terrine de Légumes de Provence

THE TERRINE
3 heads garlic
25 g (5 heaped teaspoons/
*   3½ envelopes) gelatine*
1.5 kg (3 lb) tomatoes, peeled and
*   seeded*
Salt
Pepper
4 onions, sliced
Olive oil for frying
1 eggplant (aubergine)
4 large zucchini (courgettes)
400 mL (1¾ cups) chicken stock
5 red capsicums (sweet peppers),
*   cut in large natural segments*
*   and roasted until skin blisters,*
*   then peeled*
12-16 fresh basil leaves plus extra
*   for garnish*

THE BASIL CREAM SAUCE
250 mL (1 cup) water
Small bunch basil leaves, tightly
*   packed*
200 mL (1 scant cup) heavy cream
Salt
Pepper

Serves 10

THE PREPARATION OF this beautiful appetiser takes a while, but it is easy and straightforward to make and the capsicum (sweet peppers), garlic and onions can be prepared the day before. The finished terrine sits overnight before being unmoulded, so there is no preparation on the day of entertaining.

The vegetables: Peel the garlic and cook in boiling, salted water for about 20 minutes until tender. Drain and place in a food processor. Sprinkle half a teaspoon of gelatine on top and purée to a paste. Set aside. Roughly chop the tomatoes, place in a saucepan with a little salt and pepper and cook on high heat until the liquid evaporates. This may take up to 30 minutes. Near the end, stir continuously to avoid possible scorching. When most of the liquid has gone, sprinkle with a scant teaspoon of gelatine and continue till the mass is dried out completely. Allow to cool.

Cook the onions slowly in a little olive oil for about 20 minutes until completely tender. Set aside. Cut the eggplant (aubergine) and zucchini (courgettes) into long thin slices without peeling, and in a second pan, fry the slices in olive oil until tender, but not more than lightly coloured. Transfer each slice to paper towels to drain.

To assemble the terrine: With all the vegetables ready, soften the remaining gelatine in the chicken stock. Line a 1.5–2 L (1½–2 qt) terrine or bread pan with plastic wrap, using a tiny bit of water to help it cling to the edges of the mould.

Pour about 15 mL (1 tablespoon) lukewarm stock into the bottom of the terrine and arrange a layer of red capsicums (sweet peppers) in the base, prettier side downward. The layer may contain two thicknesses of vegetables. Drizzle with a little more stock and then make a further layer with the softened onions. Pour in a little more stock, then arrange a layer of fried zucchinis (courgettes), then stock, then a layer of puréed garlic. Cover the garlic layer with a row of fresh basil leaves, a tiny bit more stock, then a layer of eggplant (aubergine) slices. Finish with a layer of the tomato purée, and then, making a few holes with a knitting needle or skewer, pour the rest of the stock over the top and tap it down into the terrine. Note that the stock should not look like a layer itself, it merely binds the layers together so the unmoulded terrine will cut neatly.

Place overnight in the refrigerator. Unmould onto a wooden board and serve sliced. For neat slicing, hold the end with a broad-bladed spatula, cut each slice about 1.5 cm (½ in) thick, tip it over onto the spatula, then transfer to the plate, easing it off the spatula with a knife. Serve with sauce and garnish with extra basil leaves.

The basil cream sauce: Heat the water to boiling, then throw in the basil leaves. Stir once, then add half the cream. Transfer to a blender and purée to a green liquid, then return to the saucepan, add the remaining cream and reduce to a light sauce consistency, seasoning to taste with salt and pepper. Serve cold.

SALAD OF ARTICHOKES AND AIR-DRIED HAM

Salade d'Artichauts et Jambon de Montagne

8 slices air-dried ham (or
    prosciutto)
4 large cooked artichoke hearts
    (either fresh or preserved in oil)
4 individual dried goat cheeses or
    150 g (5 oz) of a larger, matured
    (dried) goat cheese
8–12 cos (romaine) lettuce leaves
    plus 8–12 leaves red lettuce
    (radicchio or oakleaf) or chosen
    mesclun (mixed small-leaved
    greens)
12–16 black olives

THE DRESSING
125 mL (generous ½ cup) olive oil
10 mL (2 teaspoons) red wine
    vinegar
Salt
Pepper

Serves 4

IN WONDERFUL SUNNY weather, the best of Provençal produce — local air-dried ham, goat cheese, artichokes and black olives — combines to make this a salad that simply begs to be eaten outside.

Lightly roll the ham slices; cut the artichoke hearts in three and cut the cheese into slices. Arrange all the ingredients attractively on individual serving plates. Combine the dressing ingredients and drizzle over the salad just as it is served.

CAMARGUE SALAD

Salade Camarguaise

2 L (2 qt) boiling, salted water
500 g (1 lb) rice (Camargue rice is
    starchy, and thus, if you cannot
    find the original, it should be
    substituted with Calrose or
    Italian Arborio rather than the
    heavily washed packaged Asian
    varieties)
1 red capsicum (sweet pepper),
    cored, de-veined and finely
    sliced
2 tablespoons capers
Curly endive (frisée)
3 hard-boiled eggs, quartered
    lengthways

THE VINAIGRETTE
125 mL (generous ½ cup) olive oil
45 mL (3 tablespoons) red wine
    vinegar
1½ teaspoons Dijon-style mustard
1 clove garlic, crushed for its juice
    only
Salt
Black pepper

Serves 6

ON THE BARREN, flat marshlands of the Rhône delta, the countryside changes magically into a strange French 'Wild West', known as the Camargue. Home to pink flamingoes, herons, and a myriad other birds, the area is crisscrossed with the small white houses of the *gardians*, felt-hatted cowboys to the stocky white horses and small black toros that have given the region its fame. The Camargue's only industry, bar tourism and horseriding, is rice growing beside the marshy waters.

I first tasted this salad in a small café alongside the tiny church beloved of the gypsies in Stes Maries de la Mer.

Bring the salted water to the boil in a large saucepan, add the rice, stir once and cook until tender (about 11 minutes, depending on the type of rice). Drain and rinse in a sieve under cold water. Drain well again before transferring to a bowl.

Stir the sliced capsicum (sweet pepper) pieces and capers into the rice then, just before serving, stir in the very well emulsified vinaigrette (see below). Transfer to a serving plate and edge the rice with sprigs of curly endive and the quartered hard-boiled eggs.

The vinaigrette: Place the oil in a bowl with the vinegar, mustard and juice of the garlic. Season to taste with salt and freshly milled black pepper. Blend well with a wire whisk just before adding to the rice. The secret of this recipe is to emulsify the oil and vinegar very well to give it a creaminess akin to mayonnaise, thus adding a richness to the salad that inadequately mixed oil and vinegar cannot do.

NICOISE SALAD

Salade Niçoise

THE SALAD

1 mignonette lettuce (small red-
and green-leafed lettuce) or
150 g (2 cups) mesclun (mixed
small-leaved greens)

9 firm medium tomatoes,
quartered

6 small green onions, peeled and
cut in rings

1 large green capsicum (sweet
pepper), seeded and cut in strips

½ bunch celery, thinly sliced

12 anchovy fillets, halved
lengthways

250 g (8 oz) canned tuna in olive
oil, flaked

100 g (3½ oz) small black Niçoise
olives

12 leaves fresh basil

6 hard-boiled eggs, quartered

Optional: fresh baby artichokes,
very young broad (fava) beans,
green beans, radishes, diced
cooked potatoes

THE VINAIGRETTE

2 cloves garlic, crushed
30 mL (2 tablespoons) lemon juice
125 mL (generous ½ cup) olive oil
Salt
Pepper

Serves 6

THE MOST INTERNATIONALLY known of all regional salads, the *salade niçoise* has as many versions as there are cooks. Some may chop the vegetables smaller, some may arrange them in layers, some toss them in a bowl, some serve them without tuna . . . but all versions contain the ubiquitous black olives, anchovies and tomatoes. It's up to you to perfect your own presentation.

Line a large, open salad bowl with lettuce, then add the tomatoes, onions, capsicum (sweet pepper), celery, anchovies and tuna. Add the olives and then the basil leaves, crushed with the fingers. Pour the vinaigrette (see below) over the salad just before serving. Lastly, add the eggs, so they do not crumble when the salad is tossed.

The vinaigrette: Combine all the vinaigrette ingredients in a jar.

PAN BAGNAT

Pan Bagnat

*1 crusty round bread roll or ¼ of a
  baguette (French breadstick)*
½ clove garlic
45 mL (3 tablespoons) olive oil
*2-3 lettuce leaves (mignonette — a
  small red- and green-leafed
  lettuce — or butter lettuce)*
1 tomato, sliced
½ hard-boiled egg, sliced
*15 g (1 tablespoon) flaked canned
  tuna in oil*
6-7 black olives, pitted and halved
8 slices cucumber
*2-3 strips green capsicum (sweet
  pepper)*
3 anchovy fillets
Salt
Black pepper

Serves 1

LITERALLY 'BATHED, OR moistened bread', the name is so much more picturesque in the ancient language of the Provençaux. Nearly a *salade niçoise* in a bread roll . . . the secret is in the drizzled olive oil. Great for a picnic lunch.

Cut the breadroll or baguette in half and discard the soft crumb in the centre. Rub the bread inside with garlic. Drizzle a tablespoon or so of olive oil over the base of the inside, and rub a little over the top, making sure it is absorbed.

Place lettuce leaves on the base, adding slices of tomato, hard-boiled egg, flaked tuna, olive halves, cucumber slices, capsicum (sweet pepper) and anchovies. Season with salt and freshly ground black pepper, and add another layer of lettuce leaves. Place the top of the roll in position, cover with foil, press firmly with a light weight and stand in a cool place for 10–20 minutes before serving. The longer it stands before you eat it, the more moist and delicious it becomes.

ARTICHOKES WITH TOMATO STUFFING

Artichauts à la Concassée de Tomates

6 large globe artichokes
Juice 1 lemon, reserve lemon pieces

THE TOMATO FILLING
60 mL (4 tablespoons) olive oil
1 onion, chopped
5 large tomatoes, peeled, seeded
*   and chopped*
4–5 leaves fresh oregano or basil,
*   chopped*
Salt
Freshly ground black pepper

Serves 6

THE ARTICHOKE IS much-loved all over France and is most often eaten with the leaves dipped in vinaigrette or Hollandaise sauce. But this regional sauce gives a different perspective. Hidden in the vegetable section is the recipe for the region's prize artichoke dish, *Artichauts à la Barigoule* (page 111), also a dish with enough character to stand alone as a beguiling appetiser.

The artichokes: Trim any wilted or discoloured leaves from the base of the artichoke, then cut the stem off at the base. Sprinkle the artichokes with lemon juice and drop them into boiling, lightly salted water, with the reserved pieces of lemon. Boil until tender — usually about 30–40 minutes, depending on size. Drain well, preferably upside-down in a colander. When cool, gently squeeze the water out without disturbing the shape, then carefully part the leaves, reach down into the centre with your fingers and pluck the 'choke' (hairy centre) from the interior of the base.

The tomato filling: Heat the olive oil and cook the onion gently until softened without colouring, then add the tomatoes and oregano. If using the basil, put in half now, and half just as the cooking is finished. Bring to the boil, reduce the heat and simmer for about 20 minutes, until most of the water is reduced. Do not overcook, or the mixture becomes mushy — the tomato is not so much a sauce as a flavoursome, chunky 'dip' for the leaves and the base of the artichoke.

   Season with salt and pepper and spoon the filling into the artichoke centres. Serve warm or at room temperature. If serving at room temperature, drizzle with a little olive oil to give a sheen.

RED CAPSICUM (SWEET PEPPER) BAVAROIS

Bavarois aux Poivrons Rouges

THE BAVAROIS
*500 g (1 lb) red capsicums (sweet
    peppers), seeded and chopped*
150 mL (⅔ cup) chicken stock
*15 g (3 teaspoons/2 envelopes)
    gelatine*
*125 mL (generous ½ cup) heavy
    cream, whipped*
Salt
White pepper
Pinch cardamom

THE GARNISH
Mixed green salad leaves (mesclun)
90 mL (⅓ cup) olive oil
*30 mL (2 tablespoons) red wine
    vinegar*
*Thinly sliced capsicum (sweet
    pepper)*

Serves 4

A SOPHISTICATED STARTER to any grand meal, the bavarois needs to be prepared at least 3 hours before it is required.

The bavarois: Place the capsicums (sweet peppers) in a saucepan with the stock and cook gently for about 45 minutes until very tender. Drain any remaining liquid and purée the capsicums (sweet peppers) in the food processor or blender. Pass through a sieve to remove the skin.

Soften the gelatine in a little water, then add to the purée while still warm. Cool until it begins to thicken to the same consistency as the whipped cream, before carefully folding in the cream. Season with salt, pepper and cardamom. Line the base of four small custard cups with waxed paper and pour in the mixture. Place in the refrigerator for 3 hours to set.

To serve: Unmould the bavarois onto small serving plates by running a knife around the edge, then tapping the base. Top with a tiny slice of capsicum and surround with a little mixed salad which should be drizzled with oil and red wine vinegar.

Note: You may make the chicken stock up to 250 mL (1 cup), pour off the 150 mL (⅔ cup) needed for the capsicums (sweet peppers), then add 5 g (1 teaspoon) gelatine to the rest, and pour a small quantity into the base of each mould. This sets to give you a shiny top to the unmoulded bavarois, but is optional.

ZUCCHINI (COURGETTE) FLOWER FRITTERS
Beignets de Fleurs de Courgettes

THE BATTER
150 g (1¼ cups) plain (all-purpose)
* flour*
2 eggs, separated
15 mL (1 tablespoon) olive oil
250 mL (1 cup) milk
Peanut or grape seed oil for deep
* frying*
Salt
Pepper

30 zucchini (courgette) flowers

Serves 6

THE BEST CHEFS stuff zucchini (courgette) flowers with tiny mushrooms and steam them with truffles from Vaucluse. It is more truly Provençal, however, to serve zucchini (courgette) flowers as fritters. Stay on your toes! The flowers must be picked at their peak, cooked at the last minute, then rushed to the table. It's worth it!

The batter: Place the flour in a bowl, make a well in the centre and add the egg yolks and olive oil. Using a wire whisk, mix the ingredients in the centre of the well, then incorporate the flour a little at a time. Add the milk a little at a time. Stir until the mixture is smooth and shiny. Rest the batter an hour, then just before using, whisk the egg whites to firm peaks, and fold gently into the batter.

The zucchini (courgette) flowers: Remove any large pistils from the flowers, but wash them only if you have to, making sure that you pat them as dry as possible, or the batter coating will slip off.

When the batter is ready, heat the oil to about 170°C (340°F). Dip the flowers in the batter and lower gently into the hot oil. Cook in batches, about six at a time, allowing the oil to reheat before proceeding, and transferring each batch to a bowl or tray lined with paper towels. Keep warm.

Before serving, season flowers with salt and pepper. Serve as they are, or with a hot tomato sauce (see page 143), or a cold tomato coulis of puréed peeled tomatoes into which you incorporate a few chopped green onions, basil leaves and parsley.

ZUCCHINI (COURGETTE) FLOWERS STUFFED WITH MUSHROOMS

Fleurs de Courgettes Farcies aux Champignons

8 small zucchini (courgettes) with
the flowers in place

THE STUFFING
45 g (3 tablespoons) butter
2 shallots, finely chopped
300 g (9½ oz) cultivated button
mushrooms, finely chopped
2 tablespoons chopped parsley
Salt
Pepper

THE TOMATO SAUCE
60 mL (4 tablespoons) olive oil
2 shallots, finely chopped
4 large tomatoes, peeled, seeded
and diced
5 g (1 level teaspoon) sugar
2 cloves garlic, finely chopped
Salt
Pepper
Sprig thyme or oregano

Serves 8

ALTHOUGH MORE FIDDLY to prepare than zucchini (courgette) flower fritters (see previous recipe), this dish allows for both the vegetable and the sauce to be prepared ahead of time. A few moments in the steamer, and this jewel of Provençal cuisine can be on your table.

Wash the zucchini (courgettes), making sure you do not separate the attached flowers. Dry on paper towels.

The stuffing: Heat the butter in a frying pan and sauté the shallots until softened. Add the mushrooms, and sauté for 5 minutes on high heat so the moisture evaporates. Remove from the heat and add the parsley, salt and pepper. Transfer to a bowl, allow to stand for a moment to release the moisture, then carefully spoon out the solids only and stuff the flowers, closing in the mixture by twisting the top of the flower to shut the opening.

The sauce: Heat the olive oil in another frying pan and sauté the shallots until golden. Add the tomatoes, sugar, garlic, salt and pepper and thyme or oregano. Simmer for 20 minutes, then transfer to a food processor or blender and purée, adding enough water to make a thin sauce. Check seasoning, return to saucepan and reheat.

To serve: Place the zucchini (courgettes) in a steamer or on a tray above water, covered with foil or a lid. Steam for 10 minutes or until the zucchini (courgettes) are tender when pierced with a skewer. Serve on a bed of the warm tomato sauce.

CHICKEN-LIVER TERRINE

Terrine de Foies de Volailles

500 g (1 lb) chicken livers
20 g (4 teaspoons) salt
Pepper
½ teaspoon nutmeg
100 mL (½ cup) brandy
600 g (1¼ lb) pork neck (jowl butt)
350 g (11 oz) speck (salt pork)
2 eggs
45 mL (3 tablespoons) milk
24 peeled pistachio nuts
Leaves from sprigs fresh thyme

Makes 12–14 slices

ALMOST EVERY PROVENCAL household keeps a terrrine on hand. This country-style pâté is perfect for a family meal or a weekend luncheon outdoors.

The day before, pick over the chicken livers; discard the nerves and any sign of bile. Sprinkle with salt, pepper and nutmeg and drizzle with brandy. Cover the dish with plastic wrap; refrigerate overnight.

The next day, grind the pork neck (jowl) and speck (salt pork) together finely. Then separately, grind one-third of the chicken livers and mix with the pork. Add the eggs, milk and pistachio nuts. Blend well. Cut the rest of the livers lengthways into slices, then fold into the mixture, with the brandy from the maceration.

Check the seasoning: Fry a small spoonful until it is cooked through (it is unwise to eat raw pork) and taste it.

Place the mixture in a 1.5 L (6 cup) glazed earthenware pâté mould or loaf tin, layering the base first with a line of thyme leaves.

To cook the terrine, place it in a bain-marie (hot water bath) and bake in the oven at 250°C (475°F, Gas 9) for 45 minutes, then reduce the heat to 100°C (210°F, Gas ½) and continue cooking a further 1 hour 20 minutes. Remove the terrine from the bain-marie to cool; refrigerate at least 24 hours before cutting. Serve with crusty bread and continental gherkins (cornichons).

CHEESE PUFFS

Gougères du Soleil

THE CHOUX PASTRY
250 mL (1 cup) cold water
Pinch salt
80 g (5 tablespoons) butter, diced
150 g (1¼ cups) plain (all-purpose)
  flour, sifted onto paper
4 small eggs

THE FILLING
45 g (⅓ cup) grated Gruyère
  (Swiss) cheese
Salt
Pepper
10 anchovy fillets, diced
2 cloves garlic, finely diced
10 black olives, pitted and diced
4 sun-dried tomatoes, diced

Serves 8–10 to pass with aperitifs
  (about 40 puffs)

THESE 'CHEESE PUFFS of the sun' are similar to the famous gougères of Burgundy. Flavoured with anchovies, garlic, olives and sun-dried tomatoes, these dainty little morsels, however, are definitely a product of the south.

The choux pastry: Place the cold water in a saucepan with the salt and butter. Bring to the boil, stirring to insure the butter melts completely by the time the water boils. (Any further boiling evaporates the water, and disturbs the water/flour ratio.)

Remove from the heat and add the sifted flour, all at once. Stir well, with a wooden spatula rather than a spoon with a bowl shape, which catches the flour, then return to the stove for the count of 20, or until the mixture rolls off the sides of the saucepan and clings, in a ball, to the spatula. Remove from the heat again. Add the eggs, two at a time, stirring in each pair completely before proceeding to the next.

The filling: Fold into the pastry all the filling ingredients. Spoon into small balls on a lightly greased baking sheet, well spaced to allow for swelling.

Bake in the oven at 200°C (400°F, Gas 6) for 20–25 minutes, reducing the heat if they brown too early. Serve when a lovely golden brown, either hot or lukewarm. It is possible to make them in advance and reheat them, but as they may sit ready on the baking tray for up to an hour before baking, this is the better method, since they are irresistible served straight from the oven.

MILLE FEUILLES OF GOAT CHEESE

Feuillétés au Fromage de Chèvre

375 g (12 oz) puff pastry
15 g (1 tablespoon) paprika
250 g (8 oz) fresh goat cheese
12-14 mint or bergamot leaves,
*   chopped*
1 teaspoon chopped savory leaves
Pepper
1 large egg

THE GARNISH
Curly endive (frisée) *or leaves of 3*
*   small witlof (Belgian endive)*
40 g (⅓ cup) walnut halves
125 mL (generous ½ cup) walnut
*   oil*
30 mL (2 tablespoons) red wine
*   vinegar*

Serves 6

GOAT CHEESE, THE favourite cheese of the south, is
sandwiched here in a sophisticated puff pastry that
will enhance even the grandest of meals.

Roll out the puff pastry to a rectangle 2 mm (⅛ in)
thick. Sprinkle with paprika, fold over itself in
thirds, and roll again to a rectangle of about 45-50 cm
(18-20 in). Cut from this 12 small rectangles
(*feuillétés*).
  In a bowl, beat the cheese with the chopped herbs
and season with pepper (no salt). Garnish six of the
rectangles with the cheese mixture, leaving a 4 mm
(¼ in) border around the edge.
  Beat the egg in another bowl and brush the pastry
edges with it. Place the other six rectangles on top
and press around the edges to make sure they stick
together.
  Glaze the tops with more beaten egg, score the tops
decoratively with the tip of a small knife, and bake
for 20-25 minutes in the oven at 220°C (425°F,
Gas 7). Serve hot. Garnish with the salad of curly
endive *(frisée)* or witlof (Belgian endive) sprinkled
with walnuts and dressed with walnut oil and
vinegar.

LA TROUCHIA
La Trouchia

125 mL (4 fl oz) olive oil
1 onion, finely chopped
500 g (1 lb) green part only
    silverbeet (Swiss chard), washed
    and finely shredded
7 eggs
100 g (3½ oz) grated Parmesan
2 tablespoons chopped parsley
1 clove garlic, crushed
Salt
Pepper
100 g (3½ oz) small Niçoise olives
    for garnish

Serves 6

LA TROUCHIA, A VEGETABLE omelette from the Nice region, bears a distinct resemblance to the *tian* (see page 107). This speciality is made exclusively with silverbeet (Swiss chard).

Heat half the oil in a non-stick frying pan. Cook the onion until softened then add the silverbeet (Swiss chard) and cook 8–10 minutes; set aside until ready to use.

    Beat the eggs in a small bowl. Add half the Parmesan cheese, with the parsley, garlic, salt and pepper to taste, then the contents of the frypan.

    Heat the rest of the olive oil in a non-stick frying pan, and when warm, add the egg mixture, stirring with a wooden spatula for 8–10 minutes on a low heat until the eggs are firm. When the eggs are cooked evenly on the base, put a plate on top of the pan and turn it over, so that you have the omelette on the plate, cooked side up. Slip it back in the pan for another 3–4 minutes, sprinkling the rest of the Parmesan cheese on top. Slip it onto a serving dish, and decorate with black olives to serve.

ONION AND ANCHOVY TART

Pissaladière

THE YEAST PASTRY
*250 g (2 cups) plain (all-purpose)
    flour*
*15 g (½ oz/1 cake) fresh
    (compressed) yeast*
*125 mL (generous ½ cup)
    lukewarm water*
45 mL (3 tablespoons) olive oil
Pinch salt
*OR use your favourite pizza shell, a
    large one of around 28-30 cm
    (11-12 in) circumference*

THE FILLING
100 mL (7 tablespoons) olive oil
*1.25 kg (2½ lb) onions, thinly
    sliced*
3 sprigs fresh thyme leaves
Salt
Pepper
12 anchovy fillets
15-20 small black olives

Serves 8

THE CLASSIC ONION TART from Nice is traditionally garnished with the salted anchovies the Provençaux love so much. Although some recipes suggest making it on a shortcrust tart base, it is most often served on a yeast base akin to a pizza. Vendors in the streets bake it on huge trays, selling it from sidewalk stalls in cut portions.

The yeast pastry: Place the flour in the bowl of an electric mixer, preferably fitted with a dough hook, or in a food processor. Dissolve the yeast in the lukewarm water; blend and pour into the flour. If using an electric mixer, add the oil, a pinch of salt and beat until the dough is well blended and begins to leave the sides of the wall to cling to the dough hook or beaters. Remove from the mixer, knead into a ball on a floured surface, then transfer to an oiled bowl, cover and leave to rise for 1 hour. If using a food processor, process the yeast and flour for 10 seconds, then add a pinch of salt and the oil down the feeder. Continue to process until the dough forms a ball. If this does not happen easily, add a little water. Transfer the ball of dough to an oiled bowl; cover and leave in a warm place 1 hour to rise.

The filling: Heat the olive oil in a saucepan. Sauté the onions briefly, tossing with a wooden spatula. When the onions are well greased, but not brown, add the thyme. Reduce the heat and cook the onions slowly, stirring from time to time, for about 40 minutes, or until they have a brown sheen and are completely softened. Failure to do this results in a strong, indigestible onion flavour.

After the pastry has been left to rise for 1 hour, roll it into a circular disc about 28 cm (11 in) in diameter or into a large rectangle to fit your baking tray. Place the rolled pastry base on a baking tray. Season the onion, salting only lightly because of the anchovies. Spread the onion over the pastry base. Arrange the anchovies in a spoke pattern on the top (a grid in the case of a rectangular pizza). Dot with the black olives. Wait 15 minutes to allow the pastry to rise around the filling. Bake in the oven at 220°C (425°F, Gas 7) for 30–35 minutes.

Serve warm or cold, cut into wedges, or in the case of a rectangle, in squares.

Note: If baking in a large rectangle — on 25 x 30 cm (10 x 12 in) baking sheet — use 2 kg (4 lb) onions, increasing the number of anchovies and olives.

PIZZA WITH GOAT CHEESE, SUN-DRIED TOMATOES AND PISTOU

Pizza au Fromage de Chèvre et au Pistou

THE PIZZA DOUGH
20 g (¾ oz/1½ cakes) fresh
(compressed) yeast
Pinch sugar
60 mL (¼ cup) lukewarm water
300 g (2½ cups) plain (all-purpose)
flour
45 g (⅓ cup) rye flour (or use the
combined measurement in
white flour)
½ teaspoon salt
15 mL (1 tablespoon) olive oil
175 mL (¾ cup) water
OR use your favourite pizza shell
— either a 28–30 cm
(11–12 in) to serve 6, or
4 individual shells

THE PISTOU
1 cup tightly packed basil leaves
2 small cloves garlic, chopped
15 g (1 heaped tablespoon) pine
nuts
Olive oil
10 g (1 tablespoon) grated
Parmesan cheese
Black pepper

IN THE RIVIERA, where tourism and fashion reign, the Provençaux have joined the push to redefine the limits of the traditional pizza. Here they do so with several of their favourite ingredients — *pistou*, goat cheese, sun-dried tomatoes and black olives — to arrive at a pizza modern Californians would be at home with. The dough, too, reflects the move toward the lighter, crisper, Californian-style of pizza, but the more traditional dough of the *Pissaladière* (page 34) may be used if preferred.

The pizza dough: Dissolve the yeast and sugar in the lukewarm water. In the bowl of an electric mixer, preferably fitted with a dough hook (or, less good, in a food processor), combine the flours and salt, then make a well and add the dissolved yeast and 1 tablespoon olive oil. Incorporate the flours into the liquid with the dough hook, adding the water as it turns, mixing well until the mixture forms a soft dough.

Transfer the dough to a floured work surface and knead to a smooth, elastic ball. Place in an oiled bowl, cover and allow to rise to twice its bulk (about 1 hour), when the dough will be ready to divide into four pizzas.

The pistou: Place the basil and garlic in a food processor or blender and process to a paste. Add the pine nuts as you go. Dilute with a little oil, add the Parmesan cheese and some black pepper. Finish by adding more olive oil down the funnel to make a smooth, spreadable paste. This may be stored for up to a week in the refrigerator.

THE TOPPING
*Olive oil for brushing the dough
    (olive oil bottled with garlic for
    a couple of days is especially
    good)*
8-10 slices fresh goat cheese
*30 g (2 heaped tablespoons) pine
    nuts*
12-14 pieces sun-dried tomatoes
12-15 small black olives
8 basil leaves, shredded
Olive oil

*Makes 4 individual pizzas or one
    larger one of 28-30 cm
    (11-12 in)*

To assemble the pizzas: When the dough is ready, form it into four small pizzas. Transfer them to a baking sheet and brush each with oil or garlic oil. Spread the centre section with *pistou*, then top with crumbled goat cheese. Finish by dotting with pine nuts, sun-dried tomatoes, and black olives. Place in the oven at 220°C (425°F, Gas 7) for 8-10 minutes or until browned and sizzling. Remove from the oven, scatter with shredded basil, drizzle with olive oil and serve immediately.

NAKED RAVIOLI

Raviolis Tout Nus

THE TOMATO SAUCE

1 large onion
1 carrot
1 stalk celery
2 stalks parsley
2 sprigs basil
2 sprigs tarragon
2 cloves garlic
3 shallots
4 tomatoes, peeled, seeded, diced
30 mL (2 tablespoons) olive oil
130 g (¼ lb) pork, ground
130 g (¼ lb) veal, ground
130 g (¼ lb) beef, ground
60 mL (4 tablespoons) tomato paste
30 g (1 oz) dried boletus mushrooms
1 L (4 cups) water
Salt
Pepper

THE RAVIOLI

1 bunch silverbeet (Swiss chard)
250 g (½ lb) pork, ground
250 g (½ lb) veal, ground
Salt and pepper
Pinch grated nutmeg
200 g (1¾ cups) grated Gruyère
    (Swiss) cheese
1 bunch parsley, chopped
1 clove garlic, chopped
3 eggs
Flour for dredging

75 g (½ cup) grated Gruyère
    (Swiss) cheese

Serves 6

NAKED RAVIOLI . . . HOW much more glamorous to call them this than meatballs with silverbeet (Swiss chard). A classic dish from the Comté de Nice.

The tomato sauce: Chop the onion, carrot and celery very finely. Finely chop the herbs, garlic and shallots. In a saucepan, heat the olive oil and add the chopped vegetables and herbs. Stir and cook gently a few moments, then add the meats. Stir to mix thoroughly, then add the tomatoes, tomato paste and dried mushrooms. Pour in the water, bring to the boil, reduce heat and simmer for 1 hour, reducing the volume by half to concentrate the flavour. Season with salt and pepper.

The ravioli: Clean the silverbeet (Swiss chard) and trim, keeping the green part only. Cook in boiling, salted water for about 8 minutes. Drain and squeeze out excess moisture, then chop roughly. In a bowl, combine the meats and silverbeet (Swiss chard). Season with salt, pepper and nutmeg, add the 200 g (1¾ cups) grated cheese, parsley and garlic, then stir in the eggs. Form the mixture into small meatballs of about 2-5 cm (1-2 in) diameter, and roll in the flour.

To serve: Cook the meatballs in a large saucepan of boiling, salted water for about 8-10 minutes or until cooked. Remove with a slotted spoon and transfer to individual serving plates. Serve with the tomato sauce and sprinkle the remaining grated cheese over the top to garnish. Each dish may be placed under the grill (broiler) to melt the cheese, if desired. The most common accompaniment to the dish is boiled noodles (tagliatelle), drained and tossed in butter, chopped garlic and parsley.

RAVIOLI WITH GOAT CHEESE AND CAPSICUM (SWEET PEPPER) CREAM SAUCE

Raviolis au Fromage de Chèvre, Sauce aux Poivrons Rouges

THE RAVIOLI
*1 cup flat-leaved Italian parsley
  leaves, blanched and refreshed
  in cold water*
*20 big leaves basil, blanched and
  refreshed in cold water*
3 eggs plus 1 egg yolk
*250 g (2 cups) plain (all-purpose)
  flour*
15 mL (1 tablespoon) olive oil
Salt
Pepper

THE FILLING
250 g (8 oz) fresh goat cheese
1 tablespoon chopped curly parsley
Salt
Pepper

THE SAUCE
*30 g (2 tablespoons) unsalted
  butter*
1 small onion, finely chopped
*2 red capsicums (sweet peppers),
  cleaned and cut into strips*
Salt and pepper
300 mL (1⅓ cups) heavy cream

Serves 6

A RECIPE IN THE grand style, for which it is imperative to have a food processor and a pasta machine to make your own pasta dough.

The ravioli: Place the blanched parsley and basil in a food processor with one of the eggs and chop.

In a clean food processor bowl, place the flour, the remaining two eggs and yolk, the olive oil, salt and pepper. Process, then add the eggs and herb mixture. Remove from the bowl and knead to a ball on a floured board. Divide into four, and roll, using extra flour, through the pasta machine until a little firmer, then process through each successive roller to the thinnest setting. Lay the strips on a board, and cut into rounds of about 8 cm (3 in) diameter. Process the remaining dough in the same way.

The filling: Blend the cheese to a paste with the parsley and salt and pepper. Place 1 teaspoon mixture on one side of each pasta disc and fold one half over the other, wetting and pressing the edges to seal the now semi-circular parcels. Lay on a clean floured cloth and cover with a second cloth until needed.

The sauce: Melt the butter, and sauté the onion until translucent. Add the capsicums (sweet peppers), salt and pepper, and cook gently until tender. Remove two or three strips of capsicum (sweet pepper), finely dice and set aside. Purée the rest of the mixture. Transfer to a saucepan. Add the cream, bring to the boil, and cook to a sauce consistency. Check seasoning, and add the diced capsicum (sweet pepper).

When ready, cook the ravioli in boiling, salted water for 6–8 minutes. Drain, place sauce on each plate and arrange the ravioli on the sauce.

LINGUINI WITH SCALLOPS AND TOMATO SAUCE

Pâtes Fraîches aux Coquilles St Jacques et à la Tomate

500 g (1 lb) linguini OR

PASTA DOUGH
300 g (2⅓ cups) plain (all-purpose)
*   flour*
2 eggs
15 mL (1 tablespoon) olive oil
Salt
Pepper
Up to 45 mL (3 tablespoons) water
2 tablespoons chopped parsley
1 teaspoon chopped chives
Extra flour to work the pasta
*   dough*

THE SAUCE
60 mL (4 tablespoons) olive oil
4 shallots, thinly sliced
2 cloves garlic, chopped
3 tomatoes, peeled, seeded and
*   roughly chopped*
30–40 scallops (choose the largest
*   available)*
Salt
Pepper
15 mL (1 tablespoon) tomato paste

10 leaves basil, shredded, or
*   parsley, depending on season*

Serves 6

THIS DISH MARRIES tomatoes and scallops — a typically Provençal alternative to scallops and garlic. The former go better with linguini, the latter with spaghetti. Although commercially made pasta may be used, the directions for making the pasta are provided.

The pasta: Place the flour in a food processor with the eggs, oil and a pinch of salt and pepper. Add enough water to dampen the dough. It should begin to 'clump' but not be wet enough to form a ball above the blades as pastry does. Add the parsley and chives.

Remove the dough to your workbench and knead in some flour until it forms a ball. Divide into three and begin to process through the pasta machine. First knead one section of dough at a time through the rollers of the machine, starting at the widest setting. Pass it through this setting at least five or six times, each time dredging the strip lightly in the flour, folding it into three and pressing together well. Then pass it through each gauge until the machine is at its second thinnest notch. Finally pass through the linguini cutters on the machine. Lay the linguini on a clean floured cloth on a platter, then proceed with the remaining pieces of dough until it is all processed.

When needed, cook the pasta in boiling, salted water until *al dente*. This is a matter of seconds, unless you hang the pasta to dry, in which case it may be a maximum of about a minute. Fresh pasta such as this may be made in advance and frozen. If using commercial pasta, cook in boiling, salted water until tender, then drain.

The sauce: Heat the oil in a large frying pan. Sauté the shallots and garlic briefly, then add the tomatoes. Put the lid on for 2 minutes until the tomatoes soften. Remove the lid and add the scallops, salt, pepper and tomato paste and cook for a minute or two. Spoon out the solids with a slotted spoon; boil the liquid down rapidly to reduce to a sauce consistency.

Make a nest in each bowl with the cooked linguini; fill the central area with the scallop mixture. Top with shredded basil or parsley.

SPAGHETTI WITH FRESH HERBS

Spaghetti aux Herbes

¼ bunch parsley
1 heaped tablespoon chopped fresh
  French tarragon
15 basil leaves
1 tablespoon chopped dill
2 tablespoons chopped chervil
12–15 chives
75 g (5 tablespoons) unsalted
  butter
1 tablespoon grainy mustard
  (Moutarde de Meaux)
30 mL (2 tablespoons) olive oil
500 g (1 lb) spaghetti
Salt
Black pepper

Serves 6

LIKE THEIR NEIGHBOURS across the Italian border, with whom their history is so inextricably linked, the people of the Côte d'Azur are great lovers of pasta. Try this simple dish with fresh herbs and the unusual French-style tang of grainy mustard.

Wash and chop all the herbs and set aside. In a small saucepan, melt the butter, then add the mustard and olive oil.

Cook the spaghetti in a large saucepan of boiling, salted water until just tender (about 7–8 minutes, depending on thickness). Drain and place in a large serving bowl. Add the herbs and butter/mustard mixture. Season to taste with salt and freshly ground black pepper. Toss well, ladle into warmed bowls and serve immediately.

SNAILS, HOME STYLE

Escargots, Façon de Chez Nous

60 mL (¼ cup) olive oil
1 large onion, finely chopped
3 shallots, chopped
500 g (1 lb) spinach leaves,
   de-veined
6–8 sorrel leaves
1 bunch chervil
75 g (1¼ cups) ground walnuts
2 tablespoons breadcrumbs
Salt
Pepper
72 snails (2 small cans), drained
   and rinsed well

Serves 6

ONCE UPON A TIME recipe books read 'Go out in the early morning on a day in which there has been rain overnight and catch your snails'. Nowadays everyone uses farmed or tinned snails. Don't think only the Burgundians eat snails; the Provençaux have a myriad recipes . . . many of which includes ground walnuts like this one.

Heat the olive oil in a frying pan, and sauté the onion and shallots until softened, without browning. Roughly chop the spinach, sorrel and chervil, and add to the pan. Sauté over a high heat to reduce their liquid, then add the ground walnuts and breadcrumbs, which will bind the sauce and mop up the remaining liquid. Season with salt and pepper and place the snails on top. Cover with a lid and warm the snails for 2–3 minutes (too much cooking will toughen them). Serve immediately, with garlic-rubbed croûtons fried in olive oil if desired.

FOUGASSE

Fougasse

THE STARTER DOUGH
100 g (²⁄₃ cup) bread flour
25 g (1 oz/2 cakes) compressed
 fresh yeast
100 mL (scant ½ cup) lukewarm
 water

THE DOUGH
400 g (3 cups plus 2 tablespoons)
 bread flour
250 mL (1 cup) lukewarm water
1 teaspoon salt
30 mL (2 tablespoons) olive oil

THE FILLING
25 fresh anchovy fillets — the
 Provençaux prefer those filleted
 from the fresh or dried, salt-
 packed anchovy, rather than
 canned ones
 or 250 g (8 oz) pitted black olives
 or 2 cups grattons
 or 2 cups roughly chopped pieces
 of ham
Olive oil for glazing

Makes 2 loaves

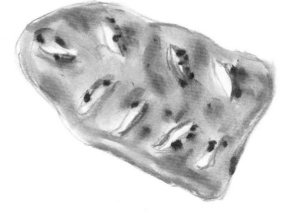

THE *FOUGASSE* OR *FOUACE* is a local Provençal bread that is fast disappearing from the households of all but the older generation, but is still found in many a proud country bakery. It is possible to find the traditionally shaped breads sold without filling, but for the most part they are baked enfolding black olives, *grattons* (deep-fried crispy bits of pork fat or duck or goose skin), ham, anchovies or even not-so-local cheeses such as Roquefort. Copiously garnished, they are like a sandwich in themselves, and one pulled apart to have with a bottle of wine in the sun makes a wonderful light lunch.

The starter dough: Place the flour in a bowl. Make a well and in it place the yeast, dissolved in lukewarm water. Stir the ingredients in the well, then gradually broaden the path of stirring to bring in the rest of the flour. Incorporate well, then leave to rise 1 hour.

The dough: In the bowl of an electric mixer, fitted with a dough hook, place the flour and salt. Make a well and add the starter dough. Mix in slowly, kneading for about 8–10 minutes. Remove the bowl, cover with a cloth and leave to rise until it doubles in volume (up to 45 minutes, depending on the room temperature).

 Turn the dough on to a floured board, knock back, add the olive oil and knead through the dough. Divide the dough in two, roll each portion out to a rectangle of about 50 x 18–20 cm (20 x 7–8 in). Scatter each with half the chosen filling, then fold the dough lengthways to form a 25 cm (10 in) long, flat loaf. Slit four or five times right through, pulling the slits wide open so they do not close during cooking.

 Brush with olive oil, rest for 15 minutes, then bake at 220°C (425°F, Gas 7) until golden, about 25 minutes.

OLIVE BREAD

Pain aux Olives

35 g (1 oz/2 cakes) fresh
(compressed) yeast
600 g (4 cups) plain (all-purpose)
flour
50 g (generous ⅓ cup) gluten flour
45 g (3 tablespoons) full-cream
(whole non-instant) milk
powder
15 g (1 tablespoon) sugar
15 g (1 tablespoon) salt
375 mL (1½ cups) tepid water
200 g (6½ oz) pitted black olives
15 mL (1 tablespoon) olive oil

Makes 2 loaves

THE RECIPE FOR this delicious crusty olive bread is from a professional baker, and is more sophisticated than the home-made olive breads that prevail in Provence. As such, it needs a good electric mixer fitted with a dough hook to do justice to its beautiful texture. If you prefer the more rustic style, choose the *Fougasse* recipe (page 44) with pitted black olives through it.

First, imagine yourself in the village *boulangerie*, and apply the bakers' rule: take the temperature of the flour and the temperature of the room and add them together. Subtract the sum you get from 64 and this is the temperature at which to bring the water to get the mixture to the perfect temperature to develop the yeast.

In an electric mixer fitted with a dough hook, place the yeast (dissolved in a minimum of the water). Mix the flour, gluten and milk powder and add to the bowl. Add the sugar and salt to the water and pour into the mixture as it turns. Mix slowly for 10 minutes, then add the olives, turn a couple more times, then remove to a floured surface and knead into a ball.

Transfer the dough to a lightly oiled bowl, cover with a cloth and leave to rise for 30 minutes. Transfer to a floured surface and fashion into two small loaves. Spray the loaves with water and dredge the tops with flour, then slash the top of each loaf three times with a sharp razor blade. Transfer to a baking sheet and leave for 1½ hours to rise again before baking. Bake at 220°C (425°F, Gas 7) for 40–45 minutes, misting the oven with a water spray at the start of cooking and again just before the end. To test the bread, remove it from the oven, turn it upside down and knock on the crust. It should sound hollow and the crust feel crispy. Cool on a rack.

SOUPS

SOUPS IN PROVENCE are incomparable. Though every region in France has its vegetable *hochepots*, its broths and its consommés and a range of puréed single-vegetable soups...Provence has soups of personality.

Even the names roll off the tongue with alacrity — *aigo bouido* (garlic soup), *soupe au pistou* (vegetable soup enriched with a fragrant paste of crushed basil), *soupa de cese* (chickpea soup), *boui-abaisso* (a spinach soup), *aigo-sacu* (a white variety of bouillabaisse).

If you want a good soup recipe, ask a grandmother — for soup making was at its height in the days of large families and housebound mothers striving to make ends meet, and her skills are unfortunately a dying art. Her soups were made from the best of the *potager* (vegetable patch), with whatever it yielded at whichever season. At its most generous, this may have been carrots or leeks and potatoes, or mixed vegetables for a *soupe au pistou*, but more often it was a handful of sorrel, one of silverbeet (Swiss chard), the head of a lettuce and a bunch of fresh herbs such as watercress and chervil. Boiled together with an onion and water to cover, passed through a sieve and poured over slices of stale bread, these were typical soups of the area.

But even the homeliest soups are enlived with olive oil-fried croûtons or aided and abetted by a good dose of grated Gruyère or Parmesan cheese; and the most peasant-like of all — water boiled with a few cloves of garlic, a little salt, a bay leaf and a spoonful or two of olive oil — *aigo bouido* — is finished imaginatively with the addition of a poached egg floating in each bowl.

With the Mediterranean lapping at its shores, Provence glories in fish stewpot soups and there is a version specific to most of the coastal areas. As any Marseillais fisherman will tell you, the quality and taste of the soup depends on the texture and type of fish available, and its grandeur on the expense you're willing to go to. A fish soup can be made of as few as three species of fish, and the flavour will change with the choice of added ingredients. Most often used are tomatoes, onions, garlic, thyme, fennel and a piece of orange peel. There are soups made of water, some with the addition of white wine (though this is heresy to a Marseillais), a *bouillabaisse riche* where fish stock is used as a base, and there is a *bouillabaisse aux poissons d'eau douce*, made with eels and freshwater fish. There is even a bouillabaisse without fish — the eccentric *bouillabaisse borgne* or *aigo-sau-d'iou* — made of leek, onion, a tomato, garlic, the ubiquitous orange peel, water and potatoes. Served like the dressiest service of plated fish in the most sophisticated bouillabaisse, the broth is poured over bread in the soup bowls, while the potatoes are lifted from the pot onto a serving platter and topped with eggs poached in the broth.

If a fish soup is not made with *rascasse* (scorpionfish, a type of red rock cod), it is strictly not a bouillabaisse but a *soupe de poissons*, unless of course it is the white-fleshed monkfish (goosefish) purée called *bourride*, so elegantly enriched to a creamy mass with aioli. And if the fish in the market is not tempting enough for a *soupe de poissons*, there is always the hope of a *soupe aux moules* (mussel soup), a *soupe aux crabes* (crab soup), or an *oursinado* (almost a *bourride*, but with the aioli thickening replaced with an egg yolk and sea urchin purée).

Just as I said…soups in Provence are never boring; soups in Provence have personality.

FRESH TOMATO SOUP WITH BASIL GRANITA

Soupe aux Tomates Fraîches et Granité au Basilic

THE BASIL GRANITA
*400 mL (½ cup plus 2 tablespoons)
    water*
30 g (2 tablespoons) sugar
Grated peel and juice 2 lemons
*2 handfuls basil leaves, finely
    chopped*
*30 mL (2 tablespoons) Pernod,
    Ricard or other pastis*

THE TOMATO PUREE
12 ripe medium tomatoes
Salt
Pepper

Serves 6

THIS UNUSUAL CONCEPT for a summer soup manages to capture the freshness of garden tomatoes and a refreshingly different pungency from its most complementary herb, sweet basil. Imagine yourself eating it on a patio in a herb-laden garden of a stone-walled *mas* in the Lubéron.

The basil granita: Boil together the water, sugar and lemon peel for 5 minutes. When cool, add the lemon juice and strain. Add the basil and Pernod. Place in the freezer. If to be served that day, stir with a fork every 30 minutes to break the ice crystals. If to be served the following day, or after, freeze in small quantities, e.g. in ice cube trays, and break up in a food processor just before serving.

The tomato purée: In a food processor or blender purée the tomatoes, then sieve to remove skins and seeds. Season with salt and pepper. Refrigerate until well chilled.

To serve: Ladle the purée or 'soup' into bowls, and serve with a scoop of the basil granita in the centre.

SUMMER TOMATO SOUP

Soupe de Tomates d'été

1 kg (2 lb) fresh very red Roma
  (plum) tomatoes
45 mL (3 tablespoons) oil or 30 g
  (2 tablespoons) butter
1 small onion, finely chopped
1 L (4 cups) water
15 mL (1 scant tablespoon) tomato
  paste
Salt
5-10 g (1-2 teaspoons) brown
  sugar
4 green onions, chopped including
  green part
4-5 tablespoons chopped chives and
  parsley
Black pepper

Serves 8

A RUSTIC, CHUNKY-STYLE SOUP with all the glories of
ripe tomatoes and thick-cut fresh herbs. As its name
implies, this is best at the height of the tomato
season.

Drop the tomatoes into some boiling water, remove
tomatoes, peel and core, then chop roughly.

In a large saucepan, heat the oil or butter and
sauté the onion a moment. Add the tomatoes and
water and bring to the boil. Simmer for 5 minutes
and taste before stirring in the tomato paste and
seasoning with salt and a little brown sugar to
reduce the acidity.

Just before serving add the spring onions
(scallions) and copious amounts of chopped chives
and parsley. Finish by coarsely grinding black pepper
over all. Spoon into bowls and serve hot.

GARLIC SOUP

Aigo Bouido

2 L (8 cups) salted water
10 cloves garlic
10 sage leaves
Optional: 6 eggs
12 slices pain de campagne, *a
    hefty, country-style bread,
    topped with grated Gruyère
    (Swiss) or Parmesan cheese and
    warmed under a grill (broiler)*
90 mL (⅓ cup) olive oil
Salt
Pepper

Serves 6

TRANSLATED LITERALLY, *aigo bouido* means 'boiled water'. A vitamin C-enriched soup in which the garlic and sage combination is believed by doting mothers and shepherds alike to ward off winter ills. A regional variation from Aix-en-Provence floats a lightly poached egg in each soup bowl.

Boil the salted water with the garlic and sage for 15 minutes or until garlic is soft. Remove the sage and garlic. Discard the sage. Mash the garlic with a fork, and return it to the saucepan with the water. At this time you can poach the eggs in the liquid if you have chosen to use them in the recipe.

To serve: Place one slice of the warmed bread at the bottom of each bowl, drizzle 15 mL (1 tablespoon) olive oil on the bread and pour 2 ladles of soup on top. If serving with the egg, remove it carefully with a slotted spoon and lay it on top of the bread before adding the broth. Season with salt and pepper.

SOUP WITH PISTOU

Soupe au Pistou

THE SOUP
225 g (1¼ cups) dried beans,
  preferably ½ cannelini, ½ red
  kidney or black-eyed peas
1 large onion, chopped
2 stalks celery, chopped
225 g (7 oz) green beans
2 zucchini (courgettes), chopped
3 large, very red tomatoes, peeled,
  seeded and chopped
100 g (2⅓ cups) angel hair, broken
Salt
Pepper
30 mL (2 tablespoons) tomato paste

THE PISTOU
3 cloves garlic
40 leaves fresh basil (don't even try
  with dried)
Optional: 1 tomato, peeled and
  seeded
60 g (½ cup) grated Parmesan
  cheese
Salt
Pepper
45 mL (3 tablespoons) olive oil

Serves 10 (this recipe is no more
  trouble to make in large
  quantities, and freezes well)

THE PROVENÇAUX MAKE a herbal paste from basil and garlic — *pistou* — similar to the Italian pesto.

This traditional soup from the Comté de Nice of mixed vegetables with a predominance of beans, truly comes alive with the fresh, pungent *pistou* whirled into the centre at the last moment.

The soup: Soak the dried beans overnight (or pre-cook a further 30 minutes). Three-quarter fill a large stock pot with salted water (about 4 L/4 qt). Add the soaked beans. Cook for 30 minutes, then add the onion, celery, green beans, zucchini (courgettes) and tomatoes. Cook for 1 hour (not too fast or you will need to replace water lost to evaporation), then add the broken angel hair, and cook for a final 10–15 minutes, or until tender. Season to taste with salt and pepper.

Add the tomato paste to taste, to reinforce the tomato flavour. At this stage the soup is not highly flavoured, but do not pre-judge until the *pistou* has been added.

The pistou: Process the garlic and basil in a mortar and pestle or a food processor until finely chopped, then add the tomato (optional). Pour in the oil little by little, continuing until the mixture becomes pasty, then add the Parmesan. Season with salt and pepper.

To serve: Add 30 mL (2 tablespoons) *pistou* to the saucepan, boil and blend with the soup a moment. The rest is passed to the guests to spoon into their bowls at the table. The addition of the *pistou* takes the soup out of the ordinary into the sublime.

BOUILLABAISSE

Bouillabaisse

THE FISH
(French equivalents follow each kind):
3-4 kg (6-8 lb) fish, chosen from the following, or the best firm, fleshy fish available:
conger eel (congre), *scorpionfish or rockfish* (rascasse), *porgy or sea bream* (brème)
Optional: Crabs, crayfish, spiny or rock lobster, wrasse, flathead or California sheepshead (roucaou), *whiting or hake* (merlan), *gurnard or sea robin* (gallinette), *red mullet* (rouget grondin), *John Dory* (St Pierre), *mussels*

THE SOUP BASE
60 mL (4 tablespoons) olive oil
2 large onions, sliced
2 large tomatoes, peeled and seeded
1 leek, cleaned and halved lengthways
3 cloves garlic, chopped
Peel of ½ an orange
1 small lemon, cut into wedges
½ bulb fresh fennel (anise) or 1 branch dried fennel weed or stalk
2.5-3 L (2½-3 qt) liquid, in the proportion of ¾ water or fish stock to ¼ dry white wine
Sprig thyme
1 bay leaf
½ teaspoon saffron threads
Salt and pepper

THE BEST KNOWN soup of the south of France, perhaps in all of France, Bouillabaisse is considered definitely out of bounds for 'foreigners' — even those from the north of France who will be told quite pointedly that they cannot make Bouillabaisse without the fish from Provence, especially the ugly little red-grey *rascasse* (sea scorpion) which is said to be essential. With a good fish market and a wide selection of warm-climate rock fish however, you have the basic ingredients to give yourself and guests a treat. But beware . . . don't ask a Marseillais fisherman to dinner. A band of his unionists once took a northern French television cook to court for not doing it right!

The fish: Make sure the fishmonger cleans and scales the fish scrupulously.

The soup: In a large casserole, wide rather than deep, heat enough olive oil to give a 4 mm (¼ in) cover to the surface. Sauté the onions until softened, but not coloured. Add the tomatoes, roughly chopped, the leek, garlic, orange peel, lemon and fennel. Stir for a moment, then add 3 ladles of either boiling water or fish stock — the latter gives what is known as a *bouillabaisse riche*, which is considered more special, but the soup is just as commonly made with water and the white wine. Boil rapidly — the fast boiling action 'fuses' the water and oil into an emulsion, rather than giving a soup with a film of oil sitting on top. Add the thyme, bay leaf, saffron, and a first sprinkling of salt and pepper.

Cook for 5 minutes to diffuse the flavour of the vegetables, then add the firmer fleshed fish i.e., the eel (cut in large chunks), the scorpionfish or rockfish, the porgy or sea bream or the crabs or lobster, if using. Boil rapidly for 5 minutes, then add the

THE GARNISH
Sauce Rouille (see page 141)
Oven-dried croûtons of baguette
  (French breadstick)
Chopped parsley for garnish
Boiled potatoes

Serves 8–10

wrasse or hake, sea robin or mullet, the John Dory, and lastly the mussels, which are cooked as soon as they open — discard any that do not open after 5 minutes. All the fish are added whole except the eel.

Reduce the heat and simmer for a further 10 minutes. Note: the fish are not entirely covered. Test for tenderness.

To serve: Take the fish carefully from the pot and lay as decoratively as possible on a large serving platter. Pass the soup through a strainer into a tureen. On a separate plate, serve the croûtons, which are traditionally rubbed with garlic. Place a dab of Sauce Rouille on some of the croûtons and float these few in the soup, then set the rest of the rouille in a sauceboat.

Toss some chopped parsley on the fish. The fish is served separately from the soup, but in a large, wide bowl so that some of the soup may be ladled over it after the soup itself has been served. Boiled potatoes are an optional accompaniment.

MEDITERRANEAN FISH SOUP

Soupe de Poissons

THE FISH

1.3 kg (2½ lb) mixed fish made up of those mentioned in the introduction, or your best selection of firm fleshy fish available . . . and the heads and bones of all. Weigh them scaled and cleaned but not necessarily skinned.

THE SOUP BASE

60 mL (4 tablespoons) olive oil
1 large onion, chopped
1 carrot, sliced
2 leeks, white part only
2 stalks fennel
3 tomatoes, peeled and seeded
1 potato, diced
3 cloves garlic, chopped
1.5 L (6 cups) water
250 mL (1 cup) dry white wine
1 teaspoon saffron threads (plus pinch powdered saffron)
Strip orange peel
30 mL (2 tablespoons) tomato paste
Salt
Pepper

THE GARNISH

Croûtons of baguette (French breadstick) fried in olive oil then rubbed with garlic
Sauce Rouille (see page 141)

Serves 8

FOR THIS SOUP, buy fish such as gurnard (sea robin), bream (porgy), hake, pike, conger eel, wrasse and rockfish. The more variety, the better the flavour. Ask your fishmonger to fillet them, but take home the bones and heads. Tied in cheesecloth and added separately, they enhance the flavour, and although this is not the typical Mediterranean method, it is a handy trick for simplifying the straining of the soup.

The fish: Wash, clean and roughly chop them. Tie the washed heads and bones into a piece of cheesecloth.

The soup base: In a large saucepan, heat the olive oil and sauté the onion, carrot, leeks and fennel slowly until softened. Add the tomatoes, potato and garlic and cook gently 15 minutes. Add the water and wine, the cheesecloth bag of bones, then the saffron threads, orange peel and tomato paste. Bring to the boil and simmer for 35 minutes, seasoning with salt and pepper.

At the end of the cooking time, discard the bag, lift out some of the fleshier pieces of fish and set aside. Put the rest through a food mill (mouli), adding the liquid as you turn. A blender or food processor will not do as good a job, although it is possible if you are absolutely sure there are no bones.

Return the sieved soup to the stove, check the seasoning. If the soup is too thick, thin with a little water, or if too thin, boil down a little. Add the crumbled fish you have set aside.

To serve: Place a dab of Sauce Rouille on each croûton. Serve the soup in individual bowls, floating a couple of croûtons in each bowl. Serve extra rouille and croûtons apart. If you prefer not to make the rouille, the croûtons may be topped with grated Gruyère cheese.

WHITE FISH SOUP

Bourride

STOCK
30 mL (2 tablespoons) olive oil
4 carrots, sliced
2 leeks, sliced
1 onion, sliced
4 leaves silverbeet (Swiss chard),
*   stalks removed*
Sprig thyme
Small piece orange peel
450 mL (1¾ cups) dry white wine
Water to cover (some cooks use
*   a light fish stock)*

1.5 kg (3 lb) thick-cut (or filleted)
*   white-fleshed fish, cut into large*
*   chunks about 9 cm (3½ in) long*
Salt
Pepper
2-3 egg yolks
12 slices baguette (fried in olive oil
*   if desired)*
Aioli (see page 140), using 3 egg
*   yolks, 6 cloves garlic and about*
*   250-300 mL (1-1¼ cups) oil*

Serves 6

THE *BOURRIDE* IS A traditional Provençal soup. A white fish soup, it is characterised by the addition of Aioli whisked into it to give a creamy look entirely different from Bouillabaisse. The main fish used is the *baudroie* (angler fish), but most fleshy white fish are fine substitutes.

In a large saucepan or stockpot, heat the olive oil and add the carrots, leeks and onion, then the silverbeet (Swiss chard), thyme and orange peel, covering with the wine and water. Simmer for 20 minutes. Strain, return to the saucepan and reduce by one-third.
   Lay the fish in the slightly cooled stock. Season lightly with salt and pepper. Bring to just under the boil, reduce the heat and simmer for 10 minutes.
   When the fish is cooked, remove it with a slotted spoon, lay it on a serving plate and keep it warm. It is served separately from the soup.
   Reduce the soup if it lacks flavour, then correct the seasoning. Moisten the bread with a little of the broth. Reserve about half the Aioli to serve separately in a bowl, then whisk into the other half a further 2 or 3 egg yolks. Ladle a little soup into this mixture, blend well and then add this to the soup pot. Stirring all the time with a whisk, and being careful not to bring the soup to the boil because this will curdle the egg, heat the soup until it thickens a little. When properly done, the soup should lightly coat the back of the spoon. Here some cooks cheat and add cream.

To serve: Arrange the bread slices in the bottom of the soup bowls. Ladle the soup over the bread. Serve the fish and the extra Aioli apart, but simultaneously. People serve themselves as they choose, spooning soup, fish and Aioli alternately into their bowls.

SEAFOOD AND FISH

IF PROVENCE USED to be a paradise for fish lovers, nowadays it is for lovers of fish with money. The French part of the Mediterranean is fished less than ever before, the yields less generous, and the result is that prize fish such as *rascasse* (scorpionfish) and *loup* (sea bass) are as expensive as meat, and often more so.

However, the Provençaux are still fish eaters and, certainly along the coast, seafood and fish are an important part of their diet, though inland it is common to have to wait for the markets to truck in fish at the end of the week. Squid, cuttlefish, scallops and small *friture* (tiny fish suitable for frying), along with *roucaou* (wrasse or parrotfish), *mulets* (mullet), *rougets grondins* (sea robin), sardines and, to a lesser extent, *rougets barbés* (goatfish) are still affordable, and frying in flour or a light batter and olive oil (particularly for seafood, small fish and sardines) is common.

Following the folk wisdom of generations, locals revere the natural product enough not to mask it with sauces. *Faites simple* (do it in the simple way) is lore, and grilling and pan frying are the prevalent methods. Fish is rubbed with oil, or garlic and herbs such as thyme, savory or fennel, and either thrown on the grill, on an outside fire, or in the oven.

Charcoal grilling is best, and in this genre, the most renowned of the barbecue dishes is *loup grillé aux fenouil* (sea bass grilled on a bed of fennel). Encased in a fish-shaped wire grill lined with a bed of dried fennel sticks, and sometimes a few stalks of greener fennel fern to enhance the smoky flavour, the *loup* is placed over the fire to cook in its fragrant nest. As substitutes, smaller fish, such as individual-portion sized whiting or garfish take to the recipe easily, and should be served simply, with the addition of a slice of lemon for juice, a sprinkling of salt and pepper when pried from their herbal bed, and a couple of boiled potatoes on the side. *Rouget barbé* (goatfish) rubbed with oil grills beautifully and loves garlic, basil or anchovy as a garnish, as does its cheaper and more common cousin, the *rouget grondin* (sea robin). One can even find special round wire racks for the grilling of the really small red mullet or sardines, another local favourite.

Sardines and anchovies are especially loved around Nice, the former as a dinner table fish, the latter a common garnish in salads, in the famous Niçoise *pissaladière*, and as *pissalat*, the spicy fermented preparation that was once the base that gave the name to this unique local tart.

The *rascasse* is becoming scarce, and it is typical to find only tiny ones. Imperative to the authenticity of bouillabaisse, it is also a favourite fish for steaming or pan-frying as a fillet.

If there is to be a garnish or a sauce on Provençal fish dishes, it's not surprising to find it derived from those flavours typical of the area. Tomato is the most likely, but sophisticated modern recipes make use also of *fines herbes* and serve the finished dish drizzled with extra virgin olive oil, olive paste or blended herbal oils.

A word of warning: the art of fish cookery is in the timing, and many a fish has been spoiled from the conscientious cook's leaving it 'just one minute to be sure...' Don't!

WARM SALAD OF MUSSELS WITH BASIL DRESSING

Salade de Moules au Basilic

30 mL (2 tablespoons) olive oil
2 shallots, finely chopped
2.5 kg (5 lb) mussels, scrubbed and
  beards removed
Black pepper

THE DRESSING
½ bunch basil plus a few whole
  leaves for garnish
2 cloves garlic, chopped
100 mL (scant ½ cup) olive oil
30 mL (2 tablespoons) vinegar
Salt
Black pepper

Serves 6

SIMPLE MUSSEL DISHES are common to all France. This summer salad from St Tropez, however, could come from nowhere but the Côte d'Azur.

In a large Dutch oven or saucepan, heat a film of olive oil and sauté the shallots a moment to soften. Add the mussels. Grind black pepper over them, cover the saucepan and steam the mussels open. Remove the mussels and take three-quarters of them out of their shells, leaving some of the smallest ones in their shells for garnish. Set the liquid aside.

The dressing: Place the basil leaves and garlic in a food processor or blender. Slowly add the olive oil and vinegar down the funnel and process until the basil is shredded, but not fully puréed. Add about 1–2 tablespoons (15–30 mL) of the mussel juice and shallots, spooning off carefully from the pot to avoid anything gritty. Add salt sparingly and a touch more black pepper.

Spread the mussels over a large serving platter and drizzle the sauce over. They may be served warm or cold. Garnish with a few more fresh basil leaves, shredded.

Note: If you would like a spicy version, shred one small red hot chilli and scatter it through the salad with the fresh basil.

MUSSELS WITH TRI-COLOURED CAPSICUMS (SWEET PEPPERS)

Moules aux Poivrons Assortis

45 mL (3 tablespoons) olive oil
1 small onion, roughly chopped
½ large red capsicum (sweet pepper), cut into pieces of approximately 1 cm (½ in) square
½ large green capsicum (sweet pepper), cut as above
½ large yellow capsicum (sweet pepper), cut as above
2 tomatoes, peeled
2 kg (4 lb) mussels, scrubbed and beards removed
Pepper
Chopped parsley for garnish

Serves 6

A BLENDING OF THREE different capsicums (sweet peppers) makes this mussel dish especially appealing to the eye.

In a large saucepan, heat the olive oil and sauté the onion. Add the capsicums (sweet peppers) and tomatoes. Toss through the mussels and add the freshly ground pepper (no salt). Cover the saucepan and cook for about 5 minutes until the mussels are open, tossing from time to time. (Discard any that are not open after 5 minutes.) Garnish with chopped parsley.

GARLIC PRAWNS (SHRIMP)

Crevettes à l'Ail

*30-32 tiger prawns (shrimp),
    peeled and deveined*
40 g (1½ tablespoons) butter
4 cloves garlic, finely chopped
*100 g (7 tablespoons) butter, cut in
    pieces*
Salt
Pepper
About 1 teaspoon lemon juice
*2 heaped tablespoons chopped
    parsley*

*Serves 6 as an appetiser, 4 as a
    main course*

EVERBODY'S FAVOURITE PRAWN dish world-wide.
Another treat that gets as much attention in
Provence is *Crevettes aux Fenouil*, fennel and prawns
(shrimp) flambéed in the favourite beverage of the
region, pastis. The method for the two dishes is so
similar that *Crevetes aux Fenouil* is included here as a
variation. Both recipes work well with scallops.

Pat the prawns (shrimp) dry with paper towels —
they will not fry well if moist. Heat the 40 g
(1½ tablespoons) butter to sizzling hot in a frying
pan. Fry prawns (shrimp) for only 2 minutes or until
opaque. They become tough if overcooked. Add the
garlic, tossing quickly with the prawns (shrimp) so it
cannot burn. Add the rest of the butter and stir until
melted. This forms the sauce, which is then seasoned
with salt, pepper and lemon juice to taste. Toss the
parsley with the prawns (shrimp), stir once and
transfer to serving dishes immediately.

Variation: Crevettes aux Fenouil (Prawns with
Fennel). Omit the garlic and replace with 2 teaspoons
fennel seed. Before adding the final butter, flambé the
prawns (shrimp) in 45 mL (3 tablespoons) pastis —
Pernod or Ricard. You may choose to change the
chopped parsley to half parsley, half chopped dill.

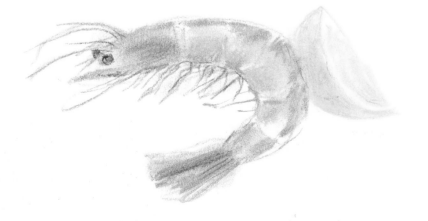

PRAWNS (SHRIMP) MANON

Crevettes Manon

90 mL (generous ⅓ cup) olive oil
120 g (¾ cup) julienne of mixed
    vegetables: carrot, turnip, green
    beans, snow peas (mange tout),
    celery or leek
30 large prawns (shrimp), peeled,
    tails on if preferred, or yabbies
    (small freshwater crayfish)
Salt
Black pepper
12 black olives, diced
2 tablespoons chopped flat-leaved
    (Italian) parsley

Serves 6

SUBTLE IN FLAVOUR and attractively presented in the modern style, this dish is dedicated to the heroine of Marcel Pagnol's popular novel *Manon des Sources*.

Heat half the oil and sauté the vegetables until they soften (1½–2 minutes). Add the prawns (shrimp) or yabbies (crayfish), cover and cook through — 2–3 minutes, depending on size. Season with salt and pepper, stronger on the pepper, then toss in the black olives and parsley just as you are about to lift them from the pan. Arrange onto small serving plates, then drizzle the remaining unheated olive oil over the dish. Serve immediately.

WARM SALAD OF TUNA AND MARINATED SCALLOPS

Salade Tiède de Thon et Coquilles St Jacques

SALAD
500 g (1 lb) fresh tuna, diced
24 large scallops, halved
  horizontally
60 mL (¼ cup) olive oil
Juice 2 lemons or limes
1 teaspoon chopped fresh ginger
Mixed salad greens (mesclun) —
  enough to make a handful on
  each serving plate. Make sure
  some are very dark, bitter
  greens, like lamb's lettuce
  *(*mâche*) and rocket* (arugula)

THE DRESSING
90 mL (generous ⅓ cup) olive oil
Lemon or lime juice to taste
Salt and black pepper
Film of olive oil for frying

THE GARNISH
Chives, cut into 2.5 cm (1 in)
  lengths
Edible flowers, preferably
  marigolds or violets

Serves 6

THE TERM 'MESCLUN', derived from the Niçois verb *mesela*, meaning mixed, has become a synonym worldwide for the mixture of salad greens typically found in the markets of southern France. In its place of origin the mix usually contains *roquette* (rocket or arugula), *frisée* (dwarf curly endive), *mâche* (lamb's tongue or corn lettuce), *feuilles de chêne* (oak leaf lettuce) and occasionally cos (romaine), red radicchio or chervil.

Although served as a salad in its own right, *mesclun* is most often a bed for grilled goat cheese or a decorative garnish. Here it is used as a bed for a modern-style tuna and scallop salad.

Between 1 and 3 hours before dinner lay the tuna and scallops on a plate and toss them with the oil, lemon juice and ginger. Arrange a nest of salad greens on 6 small serving plates.

The dressing: Combine the ingredients, tasting for seasoning.

To serve: Rub a heavy iron frying pan with olive oil, heat thoroughly, and sear the scallops and tuna *very* quickly, so they remain barely cooked in the centre. Spoon them over the green salad. Sprinkle with chives and flowers, and serve immediately.

RED HOT SCALLOPS WITH BASIL OIL

Coquilles St Jacques à l'Huile de Basilic

THE BASIL OIL
1 bunch basil
1 tablespoon capers, well drained
Salt
Black pepper
About 185 mL (¾ cup) very good
    olive oil

2 large red capsicums (sweet
    peppers)
18-24 large scallops, 3 or 4 per
    person

Serves 6

THIS STRIKING RECIPE can be prepared in advance, but needs to be cooked for 3 minutes while the guests are at the table. An ideal starter to a meal.

The basil oil (can be prepared in advance): Set aside 2 basil leaves per person for garnish, then feed about 40 leaves into a food processor or blender with the capers. Salt lightly, add freshly ground pepper, then pulse the machine, feeding enough olive oil down the funnel to form a pasty liquid. If only 125 mL (½ cup) of olive oil is needed, use the rest to brush over the scallops.

Core the capsicums (sweet peppers), and cut into long wedges. Roast quickly under a very hot grill (broiler), and peel off the skin. Using a round cutter 2 cm (¾ in) in diameter, cut the flesh into small discs the same size as the scallops. Slice the scallops in half horizontally. Alternate the scallops and capsicum (sweet pepper) discs to form a circle around the centre of white, ovenproof small serving plates.

When ready to serve, preheat the oven to 240°C (475°F, Gas 9). Brush the food with olive oil and place a ring of the basil oil around the circle of scallops. Place the plates in the oven for 3 minutes. When removed from the heat, garnish in the centre with 2 fresh basil leaves per person. Serve immediately.

STUFFED CUTTLEFISH (SQUID)

Encornets Farcis

THE STUFFING

500 g (1 lb) cuttlefish or squid
(calamari)

45-60 mL (3-4 tablespoons) olive
oil

½ green capsicum (sweet pepper),
finely diced

½ red capsicum (sweet pepper),
finely diced

1 medium zucchini (courgette),
finely diced

1 tablespoon chopped shallots

1 clove garlic, finely chopped

1 slice white bread, crust removed
and soaked in 30 mL
(2 tablespoons) milk

Salt

Pepper

10 mL (2 teaspoons) lemon juice

2 tablespoons chopped parsley

1 egg

150 mL (2/3 cup) dry white wine

200 mL (scant 1 cup) water

THE CAPSICUM (SWEET PEPPER)
SAUCE

1 red capsicum (sweet pepper),
cored, deveined, roasted and
peeled

150 mL (2/3 cup) heavy cream

Juice from cooked cuttlefish

Salt

Pepper

Serves 4

THE MEDITERRANEAN ABOUNDS in all manner of octopus, squid and cuttlefish, which are most often fried in batter. The larger the tube-like body of the cuttlefish or squid, the more likely it is to be stuffed or braised as a ragout. For this very typical dish, read cuttlefish and squid interchangeably.

The stuffing: Remove the tentacles from the cuttlefish and finely dice. Clean the interior, removing the piece of cuttle (or cellophane as in the case of squid) and set aside.

Heat the olive oil in a small frying pan and sauté capsicum (sweet pepper), zucchini (courgette) and tentacles for a moment to soften them. Transfer them to a bowl and add the shallots and garlic, then stir in the broken up bread. Season with salt and pepper and lemon juice to sharpen the taste. Add chopped parsley and bind with the egg.

Stuff the tubes of the cuttlefish or squid with this mixture, and close each with a toothpick. Place the stuffed cuttlefish in an ovenproof frying pan with a lid, and add the wine and water. Cover and bring to the boil, then transfer to the oven. Cook at 180°C (350°F, Gas 4) for 20 minutes (or simmer slowly, covered, on low heat). When cooked, transfer the squid to serving plates with a slotted spoon.

The capsicum (sweet pepper) sauce: Purée the red capsicum (sweet pepper) in a food processor or blender, add the cream, and transfer to a saucepan to reheat later. When the dish is cooked, thin the purée by adding enough of the cooking juices to bring it to sauce consistency, and to give a background taste of the seafood. Season with salt and pepper and heat. Spoon this warmed sauce over the stuffed cuttlefish.

SARDINES WITH SPINACH AND WALNUT STUFFING

Sardines Farcies aux Epinards et aux Noix

THE STUFFING
1 bunch spinach, deveined
2 cloves garlic, finely chopped
10 g (1 tablespoon) ground walnuts
100 g (generous ¾ cup) Parmesan
  cheese, grated
1 egg
Black pepper
Fresh thyme
Olive oil

40 fresh sardines or small
  mackerel

Serves 6

A FAVOURITE FISH of the Mediterranean, fresh sardines are very often floured or battered and then served deep fried. This more sophisticated recipe, however, is also very typical.

The stuffing: Blanch the spinach in boiling water, refresh it under cold water, and squeeze out excess moisture. Chop finely, and place it in a bowl. Add the garlic, walnuts, grated Parmesan and stir in the egg to bind it. Add freshly ground black pepper but no salt.

The sardines: Remove the backbone and heads of the sardines, by slitting the stomach and removing the bones with the fingers. Scale the sardines and open them out flat like a book.

Spread some stuffing onto the flesh of half the sardines, then cover each with a second flattened-out sardine. If preferred, only one sardine can be used, layered with the stuffing mixture, rolled and held with a toothpick. Oil a baking tray and place the pairs of sardines on the tray. Sprinkle with some thyme, and drizzle the tops with a little more oil. Bake for 8–10 minutes in the oven at 200°C (400°F, Gas 6).

BARBECUED TUNA WITH HERBS

Thon Grillé aux Herbes

4 tablespoons rosemary leaves
3 teaspoons fennel seed
6 cutlets (steaks) of fresh tuna, skin
   on
Olive oil
Salt
Black pepper
45 g (3 tablespoons) butter or
   100 mL (scant ½ cup) extra
   virgin olive oil

Serves 6

THIS SIMPLE BUT delicious barbecue dish is best done with fresh rosemary and fennel, but 4 tablespoons of the dried *herbes de Provence*, a blend of rosemary, sage, thyme, marjoram, basil, fennel, oregano and mint, are a fine substitute.

Lay the herbs on a board. Brush the tuna cutlets with olive oil, and press against the herbs to coat each side. Place the fish on baking paper at least 1 hour before cooking to infuse the flavour of the herbs.

   When ready, heat a barbecue, iron griddle or frying pan and for the two former brush with oil when hot. In the case of a frying pan, you will need to heat about 60 mL (4 tablespoons) oil to fry the tuna.

The tuna: Cook the tuna with the side that is most attractive face-down first (this side faces upwards on the table; more than half the cooking should be done on this side so it looks appealing on the plate). If using the barbecue or griddle, turn each piece by a 45° angle to imprint the characteristic grill marks; this is not necessary in a frypan. Cook 2½–3 minutes on the first side, about 1½ on the second side, depending on thickness. Add salt and pepper when the fish has been turned over. Do not overcook, as tuna becomes dry and fibrous. When cooked, transfer to the serving plate(s) and daub with a knob of softened butter on top of each piece or drizzle with extra virgin olive oil.

Note: The tuna may be served with grilled, roasted and peeled red capsicum (sweet pepper) and grilled eggplant (aubergine). While the tuna is cooking, place the capsicum (sweet pepper) pieces on the barbecue or griddle to reheat, and quickly dip the eggplant (aubergine) slices into oil and cook in the same way.

TUNA BRAISED IN RED WINE

Civet de Thon

1 kg (2 lb) fresh tuna, in thick
  slices
45 g (3 tablespoons) butter
12 small pickling onions or
  shallots, peeled but left whole
100 g (3½ oz) heavily smoked
  bacon (lard fumé), cut in bite-
  sized pieces
1 carrot, chopped
1 onion, chopped
10 g (1 tablespoon) plain (all-
  purpose) flour
400 mL (1⅔ cups) red wine
1 shallot, finely chopped
1 clove garlic, finely chopped
Salt
Black pepper
100 g (3½ oz) cultivated button
  mushrooms
45 mL (3 tablespoons) olive oil
2 slices stale bread, cut into
  quarters and pan-fried or
  grilled, as croûtons
Chopped parsley for garnish

Serves 4-6

IN CLASSIC FRENCH cuisine, *civet* is the name for the traditional red-wine casserole of jugged hare. Here we see the technique used with tuna, one of the preferred fish of the region, and one of the few that can be braised without falling apart. Another regional favourite, *lotte* (monkfish or goosefish) could be substituted.

Cut the tuna in large cubes as for a casserole.

Melt the butter in a casserole dish suitable for the top of the stove and sauté the small onions or the whole shallots, without colouring them. Toss the bacon pieces in also, then add the carrot and onion. Add the tuna pieces and toss a couple of times. Make a roux by adding the flour to the bottom of the pan, stir to a paste, then add the wine, the chopped shallot and the garlic. Season with salt and pepper. Bring to the boil, then reduce the heat and simmer for about 20 minutes.

Pan-fry the mushrooms whole, or quartered if large, in the olive oil. Add these just before the tuna is cooked. Spoon out the solids into a serving terrine, reduce sauce a little if necessary, adjust seasoning and spoon over the tuna. Serve the croûtons on the side of the *civet*, and garnish with chopped parsley.

BRANDADE OF SALT COD
Brandade de Morue

500 g (1 lb) boneless salt cod. If
    possible, buy the central (fillet)
    part, which is more tender
250 mL (1 cup) olive oil
1 clove garlic, crushed
200 mL (generous ¾ cup) milk
Pepper

THE GARNISH
Croûtons of fried baguette

Serves 6

KNOWN IN FRENCH as *morue*, but in many other countries as *bacalao* or *bacala* from the Portuguese and Spanish, salt cod is popular all along the Mediterranean coast. A speciality of Nîmes, *brandade* is much loved around the delta of the Rhône, but is popular throughout the region, and has become a classic dish of French cuisine.

The salt cod (advance preparation): Skin the flesh and remove any remaining bones, then cover the salt cod well with cold water for a minimum of 24 hours, preferably 48. Change the water at least 5 times during that period. On the day of serving, place the cod in a large saucepan of cold water and bring slowly to just under the boil; simmer gently for about 15–18 minutes, then drain.

In a large saucepan, heat 100 mL (generous ⅓ cup) olive oil, add the cooked cod and work well with a wooden spatula to mash the cod as you stir. Add the garlic, and, stirring all the time, alternately add the rest of the olive oil and the milk, both preheated.

The secret of the true creamy consistency of the *brandade* is the careful incorporation of the olive oil and milk, which must not be done too quickly, or they will fall from the cod as a liquid in the base of the pot. Stir well, absorbing each addition before you continue. When all the oil and milk is incorporated, season to taste with pepper. The end result should not be too salty if the cod has been well soaked.

To serve: Among families, the cod is spooned into a large oval serving dish, surrounded with croûtons of fried baguette and served from the centre of the table. A more sophisticated method is to serve it in individual, wide soup bowls, with two or three triangles of fried bread.

Variation: The Nîmois are most proud of the creaminess they can obtain from their *brandade* made from the simple emulsification of the oil and milk. However, some housewives add puréed potato to the mixture, in the ratio of about half to three-quarters the volume of the mashed salt cod. You may find you wish to double the quantity of garlic, and those not familiar with salt cod will also find this version much less salty.

MENTON COD

Cabillaud Menton

*1 large Pacific cod, ling (ling cod)
   or large white-fleshed fish of
   about 1.25 kg (2½ lb) filleted
   and skinned*

½ bunch chervil

*6-8 small black olives, pitted and
   chopped*

*4 artichoke pieces preserved in oil,
   sliced*

Salt

Pepper

*30 mL (2 tablespoons) olive oil or
   oil from the artichokes for
   cooking*

6-8 chives

*175 g (5½ oz) pâte d'olive,
   available in good delicatessens,
   OR
   15 mL (1 tablespoon) olive oil
   2 shallots, finely minced
   1 small clove garlic, finely
   minced
   200 g (6½ oz) black olives,
   pitted and finely minced*

*60-75 mL (4-5 tablespoons) extra
   virgin olive oil*

Serves 4

AN ATTRACTIVE DISH from a simple recipe in which any thick fillet of white-fleshed fish typical to your area can be used. The *pâte d'olive* can be bought bottled, but in case you cannot find it the recipe is included here.

In some of the larger white fish, including cod, there is a large central bone through much of the fillet. Place the fillets on a board and slice out these bones by running a knife along them, but take care to leave the fillet looking intact. Place each fillet on a bed of chervil sprigs, in a separate length of aluminium foil. (Save at least one-third of the chervil for the garnish later.)

Scatter the black olives and artichokes over the fish. Season with salt and pepper. Drizzle a little olive oil over each fillet. Fold the foil tightly into a package and place in the oven at 200°C (400°F, Gas 6) for 15 minutes. Roughly cut the remaining chervil, so that it still stays in fairly large, natural-looking leaves, and cut the chives into lengths of about 2 cm (¾ in).

When the fish is cooked, transfer the packages to a board, open them, and carefully use a spatula to transfer each fillet in turn to the board to slice it. Each fillet should be sliced in two, or even three. Transfer each serving piece to the plates, then scatter profusely with the chervil and chives. Place a spoonful of *pâte d'olive* near each piece of fish, and drizzle a little extra virgin olive oil over each. Serve with tiny boiled new potatoes.

The pâte d'olive: In a little olive oil, soften the shallots and garlic, then add the olives. Simmer very slowly for 1½-2 hours; pass through a sieve. Use without any liquid.

WHITING WITH BABY VEGETABLES AND PISTOU

Merlan aux Petits Légumes et au Pistou

4 small whiting (silver hake,
  Pacific hake), scaled but not
  opened through the belly. Open
  them through the back,
  removing the backbone. The fish
  will open out, with the head and
  tail holding the shape. Or use 2
  fillets of red mullet (goatfish)
  per person
About 4 tablespoons fresh, white
  breadcrumbs
Salt
Black pepper, coarsely ground
30 mL (2 tablespoons) melted
  butter
An assortment of baby vegetables,
  as the season dictates: carrots,
  turnips, zucchini (courgettes),
  green beans, onions, shallots,
  beets (cooked separately so as not
  to discolour the rest), asparagus
  tips, broccoli florets, snap or
  sugar peas (mange tout)

THE PISTOU
40-50 basil leaves
4 cloves garlic, peeled
20 g (2 tablespoons) Parmesan
  cheese
90-120 mL (⅓-½ cup) olive oil
Salt
Black pepper

Serves 4

AN UNUSUAL USE of the classic basil *pistou*. Choose your garnish from the freshest seasonal vegetables.

The fish: Place the whiting, with its flesh laid open, on a buttered baking dish, and scatter with a light covering of breadcrumbs. Season lightly with salt and pepper, then drizzle with butter. When nearly ready to serve, cook for 8–10 minutes in the oven at 200°C (400°F, Gas 6). The time depends on the size and thickness of the fish. The flesh should turn opaque, but remain moist. If using red mullet or goatfish, lay the fillets skin-side up, drizzle with butter (no breadcrumbs) and bake. When cooked transfer the fish to a serving plate.

The vegetables: Bring to the boil a pot of salted water, and add each vegetable in turn (except the beets), depending on the time they take to cook. Start with the carrots and turnips, then add the green vegetables depending on size, finishing with the snap or sugar peas. Drain and, when ready, scatter decoratively around the cooked fish. Garnish by drizzling a trail of gently heated *pistou* around the plate between the vegetables and fish.

The pistou: (This can be made in advance and stored in the refrigerator.) Place the basil, garlic and cheese in the food processor and process to a fine paste. Add the oil in two or three bursts, whir until blended, then season to taste with salt and pepper.

RED MULLET MEDITERRANEAN STYLE

Rougets Méditérranéens

6 small red mullets (goatfish),
   filleted (12 fillets) but not
   skinned
Flour for dredging
250 g (1½ cups) fine julienne of
   carrots, beans and leeks
90-120 mL (⅓-½ cup) light
   olive oil
Salt
Pepper
180 mL (⅔ cup) extra virgin
   olive oil
15 g (1 tablespoon) salted capers,
   soaked and drained
30 mL (2 tablespoons) red wine
   vinegar
15 black olives, pitted and very
   finely diced
2-3 peeled and 'turned' pieces of
   saffron potato per person (see
   page 115)

Serves 6

THIS APPEALING MODERN dish is made with *rouget barbé* (red mullet), a favourite rock fish of the region.

The fish: Rinse the fish because red mullet or goatfish tends to leave behind a few scales, then pat dry. Dredge in flour, patting off the excess. Blanch the julienne of vegetables for 30 seconds in boiling, salted water; drain well. Set aside.

Heat the light olive oil in a frying pan and fry the fish, skin-side first. Depending on the size of the fillets, they should take about 3 minutes in all. Add salt and pepper only on the second side. The first side should be crisped and lightly brown on the edges; the second needs to cook on a lower heat so it does not toughen, and more than half the cooking should be done on the first side.

Remove the fish from the frying pan and keep warm. Clean out the frying pan with paper towels, put half the extra virgin olive oil in the frying pan and add the drained julienne and capers; stir a moment. Add freshly ground black pepper, no salt. Then add the red wine vinegar, stir until boiling, then remove from the heat and add the rest of the extra virgin oil.

To serve: Place two fillets of fish on each plate and shape in the wings of a bird. Spoon the cooked julienne over the fish. Sprinkle with the chopped black olives and, if necessary, drizzle with a little more extra virgin olive oil. Place two or three pieces of saffron potato per person on the side of each plate.

SNAPPER SURPRISE

Daurade en Surprise

Butter for the foil
1.6 kg (3¼ lb) red snapper (or
*   rockfish or ocean perch) or other*
*   fleshy fish, scaled and cleaned*
1-1½ firm red tomatoes, sliced
2 shallots, chopped
75 g (2½ oz) small peeled prawns
*   (shrimp)*
Salt
Pepper
Lemon juice
Chopped parsley
6-8 sprigs basil, dill or sage (in
*   that order of preference)*
8-10 small black olives

Serves 6-8

AN INTERESTING YET simple way to deal with a large fish, with advance preparation. Vary the ingredients in the package to your choice.

Prepare a large piece of foil, one and a half times the length of the fish; butter it well. Lay the fish on top. Fan the tomato slices over the top of the fish, scatter over the shallots and prawns (shrimp). Season with salt and pepper. Sprinkle with lemon juice and parsley. Add the sprigs of herb and dot with the black olives. Butter another piece of foil to cover the fish. Place it in position and fold together the edges of the two pieces of foil to seal the package.

Place in the oven at 210°C (410°F, Gas 6½) for about 45 minutes. Open one end of the foil and test the fish at the thickest part (just behind the head) to see if it is cooked. Serve still encased in foil, removing the top section at the table.

LING CAP D'ANTIBES

Mostèle Cap d'Antibes

6 thick-cut fillet pieces (125 g,
    ¼ lb) each of ling (lingcod), or
    other large white-fleshed fish
6 large, very red tomatoes
Olive oil

THE VINAIGRETTE
125 mL (½ cup) extra virgin olive
    oil
45 mL (3 tablespoons) white wine
    vinegar
Salt
Pepper
2 tablespoons chopped parsley
2 tablespoons chopped chives
2 green onions, sliced

Serves 6

TO RETAIN THEIR garden-fresh flavour, the tomatoes in this recipe are warmed through rather than cooked, and serve as a bed for a pearly white fish fillet garnished with olive oil and fresh herbs. The colours in the end result are quite riveting.

The tomatoes: Peel, core and seed them, then cut into fleshy cubes of about 1 cm (½ in). Put a film of oil in a wide saucepan; set the tomatoes on top, cover and set aside.

The vinaigrette: In a bowl, combine the olive oil and vinegar. Season with salt and pepper to taste. Set the herbs and green onions nearby on a saucer, but combine only at the moment of serving to prevent discolouration.

To assemble the dish: Steam the fish until tender, approximately 10 minutes, depending on thickness of the pieces. Test that the fish is milky white and opaque, but do not overcook or it will become fibrous. At the same time, place the tomatoes on a low burner, to heat through, about 3–4 minutes, without cooking too much so they retain their flavour. Turn once.

To serve: Spoon the tomatoes onto the serving plates, making a bed in the centre of each plate. Remove the fish with a spatula and wipe the base with paper towels or a clean cloth to remove excess moisture. Place a piece of fish in the centre of each bed of tomatoes. Add the fresh herbs and green onions to the vinaigrette, and spoon cold over the warm fish.

SKATE WITH TWO-COLOURED CAPSICUM (SWEET PEPPER) SAUCE

Aile de Raie, Sauce aux Deux Poivrons

1.25 kg (2½ lb) skate (ray)
2 large red capsicums (sweet
*   peppers)*
2 large green capsicums (sweet
*   peppers)*
4 shallots, finely chopped
100 mL (⅓ cup) wine vinegar
60 mL (4 tablespoons) heavy cream
Salt
Pepper

Serves 4

A NOT-SO-CLASSIC PRESENTATION of a fish that everyone loves because it is bone free. If you prefer to use one sauce only, the red does the fish more justice.

Cut the skate into individual portions of around 300 g (9½ oz). Soak in water for 1 hour, to remove any sand and to whiten the flesh.

The sauces: Blanch the capsicums (sweet peppers) in boiling water for 10 minutes; remove with a slotted spoon to drain. Slice some pieces of each colour for the garnish and, discarding the core and veins, finely chop the rest, keeping the colours separate.

Start the sauces by putting half the vinegar and chopped shallots into each of two small saucepans and reducing each until there is only 15 mL (1 tablespoon) of liquid, and the shallots are softened. Into each of the saucepans place one of the colours of capsicum (sweet peppers), and 30 mL (2 tablespoons) cream. Simmer for 2 minutes, then purée separately. Return each to its own saucepan and season with salt and pepper. Reheat when needed.

The fish: The skate may be either steamed or boiled. If steaming, allow 7–8 minutes over the boiling water; if boiling, place in water at a rolling boil, reduce the heat and simmer for 4–6 minutes, depending on the thickness of the cut.

To serve: Spoon some sauce of each colour onto each plate, and place the fish in the centre where the colours meet. Garnish with the reserved capsicum (sweet pepper) strips of each colour.

POULTRY AND MEAT

LAMB IS THE predominant meat of Provence, cultivated on the hillside pastures of the lower Alpes and along the Durance River around the lamb-breeding capital of Sisteron, where it gets its distinctive flavour from wild thyme, savory and other herbal grasses of the *maquis* scrubland, rendering it rival to that other great lamb of France, the *pré-salés* fed on the salty marshes of the tidal-covered fields around Mont St Michel in Normandy.

Lamb is preferred young, and is served rare, but mutton, too, is cooked as a braising or stewing meat. Prime cuts are grilled and roasted, braising cuts stewed, made into *daubes* (long-simmered casserole dishes), and packed into iron dishes with root vegetables and cooked long and slow, traditionally over coals (whence comes the name of the cooking vessels — the *braisières*, meaning dish to be placed among the brazes) as *estouffades*, dishes particularly popular in the Camargue region.

No cut is wasted, and the Provençaux are fond of rolled stuffed roasts of shoulder, offal and variety meats (kidneys are a choice morsel), tripe, tongue, liver and *pieds et paquets*. *Gras-double* (tripe) *à la Provençale* (of beef as well as lamb) is cooked with smoked pork belly, tomatoes and herbs and finished with a garlic and chopped parsley *persillade*. It is also boiled and served with vinaigrette, and fried as fritters, as are lamb's trotters, which are also appreciated stuffed and fried. More famous are the *pieds et paquets à la Marseillaise*, lamb's trotters stuffed with tripe and meat flavoured with garlic and parsley, and made into small parcels that are layered in a casserole and braised in tomato, white wine and stock.

The sparse Provençal vegetation and small land holdings are not conducive to cattle production, but beef is a popular meat. In the marshy delta of the Rhône in the Camargue region, the small black toros bred ostensibly for the bull ring are sold as 'wild' meat at the local butcher's — an oddity, and a little tough at that, and scarcely worthy of export, even to neighbouring cities.

If *steak-frites* is of national popularity, the region's own speciality is the *daube*. The best *daubes* are made with beef cuts full of tendon and muscle — preferred is the ox cheek, or failing that, the highly gelatinous shank (gravy beef). The long-simmering cooking process — which requires no patience, just time, for the pot cooks on the corner of the stove and needs no attention — is designed to work miracles upon these morsels, breaking down the gristle into the wondrous sweet jelly that softens the meat and imparts the syrupy richness to the sauce. The authentic *daube* is never thickened; the juices of the meat simply combine with the wine and the earthy subtlety of root vegetables and herbs, and when the alchemist's work is done, the flavoursome liquor is simply boiled down until it reaches a sauce consistency.

The classic *daube* is served with the root vegetables that have seen their time in the pot...and can be finished with any number of different additions, though the most traditional is black olives. The chapter gives a traditional one and a modern, up-market version, with the added eye-appeal of freshly boiled baby vegetables.

Poultry, once cultivated in the yard and now cheap and affordable, is on everyone's table. Hunting, however — formerly almost a necessity for the poor to extend their diet — remains popular, and the wild rabbit, hare, guinea fowl, partridge, duck and small birds of the *maquis* are still regular additions to the Provençal meal.

CHICKEN WITH HERBS AND ROASTED GARLIC

Poulet aux Herbes et à l'Ail Rôti

3 heads garlic, unpeeled
1.8-2 kg (3½-4 lb) chicken
5 sprigs fresh rosemary
Good handful fresh sage leaves
250 mL (1 cup) olive oil
50 g (3 tablespoons) butter
Salt
Coarsely ground black pepper

Serves 6

A SIMPLE ROASTED chicken dish, but with such a pungent difference.

Pull 3 cloves from the garlic; peel them, rub them over the outside of the chicken, then place them into the central cavity, along with 1 small sprig rosemary and 3 sage leaves. Drizzle the chicken with olive oil, season with salt and pepper, then press the leaves of 3 sprigs of rosemary against the flesh. Stand the chicken on an oiled baking tray and bake at 180°C (350°F, Gas 4) for 1¼ hours.

Peel off the outer layer of skin from each head of garlic, hold firmly between the two hands and twist slightly. Whilst they should still hold together, this will loosen the cloves, and allow them better exposure to the heat. Rub them well with olive oil, then place in the baking tray around the chicken for the last 30 minutes of cooking time, pouring the rest of the oil over them. Turn them occasionally, so they brown evenly and do not catch or scorch, at the same time basting the oil in the base of the tray over the chicken.

After this time, remove the garlic and keep warm, then raise the heat of the oven to 220°C (425°F, Gas 7) for a further 5–10 minutes, to brown and crisp the skin of the chicken. When cooked, remove the chicken to a serving platter and surround with the cooked cloves of garlic. Heat the butter in a small frying pan or saucepan, toss in the leaves of the remaining sprigs of rosemary and sage leaves and then spoon the fresh herbs over the breast. Sprinkle with black pepper and carve at the table.

To eat the garlic, simply hold the wider end of each clove with a fork and use your knife to press the softened garlic flesh from its shell. Serve with potatoes and roasted red capsicum (sweet pepper).

BUTTERED CHICKEN WITH THYME

Poulet au Thym

2 chicken pieces per person; use
    breast (on the bone), thigh and
    drumstick pieces (no wings)

FOR 12 PIECES
150 g (10 tablespoons) butter
30 mL (2 tablespoons) oil
Juice 1 lemon
Salt
Pepper
6-8 sprigs fresh thyme (dried will
    not do)
1 teaspoon powdered sweet paprika

Serves 6

A HANDY FAMILY recipe made with pre-cut chicken pieces, but definitely attractive enough to feed guests. The thyme may be replaced with savory, or, for a very different flavour, with sprigs of fresh tarragon.

Place chicken pieces in an ovenproof rectangular dish. Dot with the butter, and drizzle with oil and lemon juice. Season to taste with salt and pepper. Place the sprigs of thyme here and there, sprinkle all lightly with paprika. Cook in the oven at 220°C (425°F, Gas 7) for 35 minutes. During this time, spoon the melted butter over the chicken pieces twice. Serve directly from the dish, spooning the butter over as a sauce.

CHICKEN BREAST STUFFED WITH ZUCCHINI (COURGETTES)

Suprêmes de Volaille Farcies aux Courgettes

THE FILLING
15 g (1 tablespoon) butter
3 shallots, finely chopped
3 zucchini (courgettes), grated
2 tablespoons chopped parsley
1 tablespoon marjoram
15 g (1 tablespoon) grated
   Parmesan cheese
Salt
Black pepper, coarsely ground

THE SAUCE *(optional)*
250 mL (1 cup) heavy cream
Salt
Pepper

3 whole breasts of chicken, boned,
   halved and trimmed to make
   tidy fillets (leave the skin on)
35 g (2 tablespoons) butter for
   frying

Serves 6

NOT MUCH CREAM is eaten in Provence, but the cream in this recipe both softens and enriches the sauce. A stronger version may be made by omitting the cream and finishing the sauce with chopped garlic, half a teaspoon of fresh thyme leaves and a little chicken stock.

The filling: Heat the butter in a small frying pan and sauté the shallots and zucchini (courgettes) for 1 minute to evaporate the juices. Transfer to a bowl, add parsley, marjoram and Parmesan. Season with a little salt and much coarsely ground black pepper.

Make a pocket under the skin of each chicken fillet with your fingers. Insert spoonfuls of the filling into the pocket; press the skin back into place and seal with 2 or 3 toothpicks.

In a large frying pan, heat the butter and lightly brown the fillets on the skin side. Turn, reduce heat, cover with a lid and cook for a further 8 minutes on the second side. Transfer the fillets to warm serving plates.

The sauce (if using): Remove excess fat from the frying pan, place on the heat and deglaze the pan with the cream, stirring up the sediment on the base of pan to enrich the sauce. Reduce to sauce consistency. Season to taste and spoon over the fillets.

CHICKEN OR DUCK ESTEREL

Poulet ou Canard Esterel

1.6-1.8 kg (3¼-3½ lb) chicken
   or duck
100 mL (⅓ cup) olive oil
Salt
Pepper
8 large, very red tomatoes, peeled
   and seeded
3 sprigs fresh oregano or marjoram
1 clove garlic, finely chopped
15-20 small black olives
125 mL (½ cup) dry white wine
1 tablespoon chopped parsley for
   garnish

Serves 6

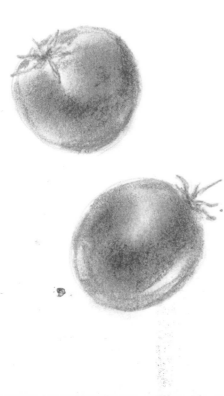

THIS RECIPE, TYPICAL of the Côte d'Azur, is interchangeably made with chicken or duck. Only the timing differs. It is best in summer when tomatoes are at their peak.

Prepare the chicken or duck for roasting. Rub with oil, then spread about 30 mL (2 tablespoons) oil in the base of the roasting dish. Season the bird with salt and pepper and roast in the oven at 220°C (425°F, Gas 7) — the chicken for 50 minutes, the duck for 1½ hours. As the duck takes much longer to cook, reduce the heat to 200°C (400°F, Gas 6) after 15 minutes, and if the duck needs further browning or crisping, return to 220°C (425°F, Gas 7) for the last 15 minutes.

Chop the tomatoes roughly and place in a bowl with the sprigs of oregano or marjoram and the garlic folded through them. When the chicken or duck is 20 minutes from the end of cooking time, remove the roasting dish from the oven and pour off *all* the fat. Spoon the tomato mixture around the bird, intersperse with olives, pour the wine over the top, season lightly with salt and pepper and return to the oven.

When the bird is cooked, place it on a board. Stir the tomato mixture and, if very liquid, place on the stove and reduce. Place the bird in a large oval dish for serving, and surround with the tomatoes and olives. Sprinkle with chopped parsley and carve at the table.

DUCK BREAST STUFFED WITH HAM AND SUN-DRIED TOMATOES

Suprêmes de Canard au Jambon de Montagne

Aquidneck
market
8.99

4 large duck breasts, without
   wings, skin intact

THE STUFFING
8 large spinach leaves
60 mL (4 tablespoons) olive oil
Salt
Black pepper
5–8 slices air-dried ham or
   prosciutto
225 g (7 oz) very lean chicken,
   ground
6 large sun-dried tomatoes, diced
2 small cloves garlic, finely chopped
1 tablespoon chopped fresh
   tarragon leaves

Serves 4

THE SHARP FLAVOURS of air-dried ham, garlic and sun-dried tomatoes in this dish provide an unusual contrast to the richness of the duck fillet. The stuffing is best placed in the fillets at least a couple of hours in advance, not only to make life a little easier for the cook, but also so the fillets hold their shape better whilst frying.

The stuffing: Pan-fry the spinach leaves in a film of olive oil. Season with salt and pepper then drain on paper towels. Finely chop one slice of ham and trim the remaining slices. In a bowl, combine the chicken with sun-dried tomatoes, the finely chopped ham and any trimmings, the garlic, tarragon, salt and freshly ground black pepper. Shape the mixture into four patties the length of a duck fillet and pan-fry the patties in a little olive oil. When cooked (3–4 minutes), remove and roll them up first in the spinach leaves and then the trimmed ham slices. Stuff these patties under the skin of the duck breast and re-form the skin over the breast. When the duck flesh is well dried, it should stick with no need for stitching; if there is not enough breast skin, it can be held in place with two toothpicks per breast.

To cook the duck: Fry skin-side down in a film of olive oil in a large cast-iron frying pan, about 10 minutes on the first side to crisp the skin and render its fat, and about 3 minutes on the underside to finish the cooking.

SAUTE OF RABBIT WITH GARLIC AND THYME

Lapin Sauté à l'Ail

100 mL (⅓ cup) olive oil
2 small rabbits totalling about
*   1.6-2 kg (3¼-4 lb), cut into*
*   portions*
Salt
Pepper
3 tomatoes, peeled, seeded and
*   diced (optional)*
2 teaspoons fresh thyme leaves
*   and/or sprigs*
2 small bay leaves
2 cloves garlic, finely chopped
2 tablespoons parsley
Juice 1 lemon

Serves 6

IN THE SOUTH OF FRANCE, hunting is extremely popular, though the rabbits may not be as prevalent in the *maquis* as they used to be. In truth, domestic rabbits suit this dish better than wild, for they are less sinewy — but then, who am I to disappoint the hunter? The addition of the tomatoes is optional.

Heat the olive oil in a flameproof casserole dish or frying pan with some depth. Brown the rabbit portions on each side. Season with salt and pepper. Add the tomatoes (if using), thyme and roughly broken bay leaves. Do not cover, but reduce heat and cook slowly, turning frequently, for about 40 minutes, or until the meat can be pierced readily with a skewer.

When the meat is tender, add the garlic, parsley and lemon juice. Serve immediately, with sliced sautéed zucchini (courgettes) or diced potato, boiled, drained and sautéed lightly in olive oil.

Variation: The French sauté is a style of dish that the uninitiated may find tougher than liquid-bathed casserole dishes. If desired, 150 mL (⅔ cup) dry white wine and 100 mL (⅓ cup) water or chicken stock may be added after the bay leaves, a lid placed on the pan and the dish left to simmer gently. The result is not the same, but somewhat more tender.

LEG OF LAMB, HOME STYLE

Gigot d'Agneau Ménagère

2 kg (4 lb) leg of lamb
3 cloves garlic, halved (and
  rosemary and anchovy if desired
  — see introduction), if studding
  the lamb; none if making the
  crème d'ail
Salt
Freshly ground black pepper
60 mL (4 tablespoons) olive oil
2 sprigs rosemary
150 mL (²⁄₃ cup) water
100 mL (¹⁄₃ cup) white wine
30 g (2 tablespoons) butter

THE GARLIC CREAM SAUCE
  (optional)
30 cloves garlic, peeled
1 small potato, peeled and cubed
45 mL (3 tablespoons) milk or
  cream

Serves 6

THE SOUTHERN FRENCH cook studs lamb with garlic and places a sprig of rosemary in the base of the baking dish. Every cook, however, has their own *façon* — some stick rosemary into the slits with the garlic, some place garlic, rosemary and slivers of anchovy in the slits. Some lovers of garlic prefer not to stud the roast at all, but to enrich their sauce with a *crème d'ail* (creamed garlic). It's your choice . . .

The lamb: If studding the lamb with garlic, make fine slits in the fleshier parts of the lamb and insert the garlic. If making the garlic cream sauce, omit this step, and rub the top of the lamb with garlic. In either case, rub the top of the lamb with salt, and sprinkle with pepper. Place in a baking dish and drizzle with the olive oil. Place the rosemary sprigs in the base, and roast in the oven at 220°C (425°F, Gas 7) for 40–50 minutes. This is rare; add 30–45 minutes if you prefer it more cooked. After 1 hour, pour off the rendered lamb fat and add the water to the dish.

The garlic cream sauce: Simmer the garlic cloves in salted water for 5 minutes. Change the water, add the potato, and cook until both are very tender (15–18 minutes). Drain, press through a sieve into a bowl, stirring in the milk or cream. Set aside.

To serve: When the lamb is cooked, remove it to a serving plate, and keep it warm while making the sauce. Place the baking dish on the stove, add the wine and replace any water that has evaporated. Stir to the boil, scraping any sediment from the base of the pan. If not using the garlic sauce, remove the rosemary, stir in the butter, season and serve in a sauceboat. If using the garlic sauce, stir in the garlic purée before adding the butter. Season, and serve.

ROLLED ROAST LAMB WITH PROVENCAL HERBS

Rôti d'Agneau aux Herbes de Provence

THE STUFFING
30 g (1 oz) shallots, finely chopped
30 g (2 tablespoons) butter
50 g (¾ cup) white breadcrumbs
150 mL (⅔ cup) lamb or beef stock
2 cloves garlic, finely chopped
60 g (½ cup) fleshy black olives,
    pitted and chopped
2 teaspoons rosemary, chopped
2 teaspoons wild thyme, chopped
2 teaspoons savory, chopped
1 egg
Salt
Pepper

2 kg (4 lb) leg of lamb, tunnel
    boned (but not butterflied) or
    you may use a boned shoulder

Serves 8

IF WILD HERBS are a delightful feature of the Provençal countryside, they are also an overwhelming feature of the regional cooking. Herbs grow in gardens and are plucked fresh, they stand in vases throughout the house, and hang in bunches to dry around the window frames and from chimney ledges. Here fresh herbs join black olives as the stuffing for a boned leg of lamb. Though fresh herbs give a moister result, the dish may be done with dried *herbes de Provence.*

The stuffing: Sauté the shallots in butter. Soak the bread in the lamb or beef stock for 5 minutes. Place in a bowl with the garlic, olives and herbs. Beat the egg and mix in, then season with salt and plenty of pepper.

The lamb: Insert the stuffing into the bone cavity of the lamb. If using a shoulder, spread stuffing over the surface of the meat, then roll. Tie firmly. Bake for 1 hour in the oven at 200°C (400°F, Gas 6) (the shoulder will need 1½ hours). Rest for 10 minutes before cutting the strings and carving into thick slices.

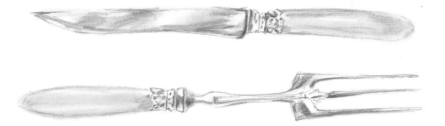

CARTWHEEL OF LAMB WITH BABY VEGETABLES

Bûche d'Agneau aux Petits Légumes

*2 boned loins of lamb weighing
750–850 g (1½–1¾ lb), keeping
both the larger fillet of each,
and the smaller*
*2–3 teaspoons sun-dried tomato
paste*
About 16 sun-dried tomatoes
Olive oil
Salt
Pepper

THE VEGETABLES
*Depending on the season, choose
enough baby vegetables to feed
8 people generously: carrots and
turnips, eggplant (aubergine)
and zucchini (courgettes), green
beans and/or sugar peas (mange
tout), summer squash,
asparagus tips, green onions,
fresh corn, fennel (anise) and
artichoke*
Olive oil for cooking
Salt
Pepper
2 tablespoons chopped parsley

THE SAUCE
200 mL (1 scant cup) white wine
*200 mL (1 scant cup) water, lamb
or chicken stock*
1 teaspoon sun-dried tomato paste
Salt
Pepper

Serves 8

THE SECRET OF this dish is the unusual manner of rolling and stuffing the prime loin cut, and serving it on a nest of baby seasonal vegetables braised in olive oil.

To prepare the meat: Remove any fat, sinew or gristle from the large 'eye' sections of the loin, butterfly them lengthways and open them out like a book. Flatten a little with a meat mallet. Lay one section on a board and slightly overlap the first with the second. Paint the meat with sun-dried tomato paste. Cover the paste with basil leaves, laying them flat over the entire surface. Place a layer of sun-dried tomatoes on this. Lay the two smaller lamb fillets in the centre and roll the meat firmly into a loaf. Tie securely with string along the length. Brush with olive oil and set aside in a roasting pan for 1–2 hours to help firm the shape of the roll.

When ready to cook, sprinkle with salt and pepper and bake in the oven at 240–250°C (475–500°F, Gas 8–9) for 18 minutes; remove, keep it warm, and rest for 7–10 minutes before untying the strings and carving into thick 1 cm (½ in) slices.

The vegetables: Peel the carrots and turnips, leaving a little of the green. Trim the ends off the eggplant (aubergine) and zucchini (courgettes), green beans and/or sugar peas or trim any other vegetable if necessary. The vegetables take just about the same time as the meat. Heat 5 mm (¼ in) olive oil in a wide frying pan and toss the vegetables until they are lightly oiled. The carrots, depending on size, may take 4–5 minutes longer than the rest, but normally all except the sugar peas can be cooked together for the whole 18 minutes. Reduce the heat and place a lid on the saucepan, then braise gently in the oil until tender, adding the peas only for the last 2–3 minutes. Finish with salt, pepper and chopped parsley.

The sauce: While the meat is resting, add the white wine to deglaze the roasting dish, and the water, or lamb or chicken stock. Stir in the tomato paste. Bring to the boil, stirring to pick up all the meat sediment. Season to taste with salt and pepper.

To serve: Divide the vegetables among the plates. There should be enough to give a generous nest of vegetables on each plate. Cut the meat and place two pieces of meat per person on top of the vegetables. Spoon a couple of spoonfuls of sauce over the edge of the meat and onto the plate; serve the rest at the table.

RACK OF LAMB WITH PASTIS BUTTER

Carré d'Agneau au Beurre de Pastis

THE EGGPLANT (AUBERGINE)
   GATEAUX
4 zucchini (courgettes)
45 mL (3 tablespoons) olive oil
1 kg (2 lb) eggplants (aubergines),
   unpeeled, diced
Salt
Pepper
2 cloves garlic, finely chopped
1 teaspoon thyme
1 bay leaf
3 eggs
15 mL (1 tablespoon) milk

THE PASTIS BUTTER
200 g (3¼ cups) soft breadcrumbs
3 cloves garlic, finely chopped
150 g (10 tablespoons) butter
2 tablespoons finely chopped parsley
Salt
Pepper
30 mL (2 tablespoons) Pernod,
   Ricard or other pastis

THE LAMB
2 large 6-chop racks of lamb or
   1 small 3-chop rack per person
15 mL (1 tablespoon) olive oil

BASED ON THE classical dish *Carré d'Agneau Persillé*, but with the addition of pastis, that omnipresent aperitif of the south, this *carré* becomes unmistakably Provençal. The eggplant (aubergine) gâteaux serve as an attractive garnish and may be used to accompany other strong-flavoured meats.

The eggplant (aubergine) gâteaux: (These can be cooked in advance and reheated.) Cut the unpeeled zucchini (courgettes) into thin 1.5 mm (¹⁄₁₆ in) slices along their length. Heat a small film of olive oil in a frying pan and toss the zucchini (courgettes) in the oil for a moment, without colouring, to soften them. Remove and line the top and sides of 6 x 125–150 mL (½ cup) custard cups with the slices.

Sauté the diced eggplant (aubergine) slowly for 15 minutes in 30 mL (2 tablespoons) olive oil. Season with salt and pepper. Add the garlic, thyme and bay leaf, cover the pan and cook a further 15 minutes. Drain off excess moisture, remove the bay leaf and purée the mixture in a blender or food processor, adding the eggs and milk. Check the seasoning, then spoon the purée into the zucchini- (courgette-) lined custard cups, fold any overhanging strips of zucchini (courgette) back over the purée, and place the ramekins in a bain-marie. Bake in the oven at 200°C (400°F, Gas 6) for 35 minutes, the top of the custard cups covered with a sheet of buttered baking parchment.

The pastis butter: In a food processor or blender, combine the breadcrumbs and the garlic, chop finely, then add the butter and parsley. Season with salt and pepper and flavour to taste with the pastis.

THE SAUCE
100 g (7 tablespoons) butter
1 tablespoon chopped shallots
2 heaped tablespoons very finely
  diced black olives
1 tablespoon finely chopped parsley

Serves 6

The lamb: Bake the lamb for 18–20 minutes
(depending on size and age) at 240°C (475°F, Gas 8).
When cooked, remove from the oven and spread the
pastis butter mixture on the back of the racks. Place
under the griller (broiler) for a few moments.

To serve: Place the racks, cut into chops or left whole,
as dictated by the size, onto the serving plates.
Unmould the eggplant gâteaux onto the plates beside
the lamb.
  Heat the butter for the sauce in a small saucepan
and toss the shallots a moment to soften them.
Add the olives and heat them, then add the parsley.
Spoon the sauce over the eggplant gâteaux.

LAMB WITH EGGPLANT (AUBERGINE) RAGOUT
Côtelettes d'Agneau au Ragoût d'Aubergines

THE EGGPLANT (AUBERGINE) RAGOUT

8 Japanese eggplants (aubergines), cut in two lengthways, or 1 long thin one, cut into strips
90 mL (⅓ cup) olive oil
2 small yellow onions, diced
1 teaspoon coriander seeds
1 red chilli
About 12–14 spinach leaves
Salt
Pepper

THE JUS

25 g (2 tablespoons) butter
100 g (3½ oz) lean lamb from leg or shoulder, diced
600 mL (2½ cups) strong lamb stock
Pinch fennel or coriander seed
The 'essence' of the lamb sediment (see recipe)
Salt
Pepper
15 g (1 tablespoon) butter

THE MEAT

45 g (3 tablespoons) butter
45 mL (3 tablespoons) olive oil
3 double lamb loin chops, trimmed, chine bone removed and only the rib bone left in
Salt
Pepper

Serves 6

A PRIME MORSEL from the most prized meat of the area served here with a spicy eggplant (aubergine) dish. The eggplant (aubergine) and spinach ragout would just as admirably sit beside a prime steak.

The eggplant (aubergine) ragout: Brush the cut sides of the eggplants (aubergines) with olive oil. Place the eggplants (aubergines) under the griller (broiler) until brown. Cool and cut into 2 cm (¾ in) lengths. Heat the remainder of the olive oil in a saucepan. Add the onions and coriander seeds. Fry the onions slowly for 5 minutes, without browning, then add the eggplants (aubergines) and chilli. Cook the mixture until softened a little (5 minutes) then stir in the spinach leaves until they just wilt (30 seconds). Season with salt and pepper.

The jus: In a saucepan, heat the butter and brown the diced lamb well. Add 125 mL (½ cup) stock and reduce to a glaze on the pan. Repeat this, then add the rest of the stock and the spice, bring to the boil and reduce to sauce consistency. Set aside until the lamb is cooked, then add the 'essence' of the cooked lamb. (After removing the lamb, add a little water to the frying pan. Simmer on the stove, scraping up the sediment.) Season with salt and pepper and whisk in the butter.

The meat: In a frying pan, heat the butter and oil and fry the chops until browned, but pink on the inside (3–4 minutes). Season with salt and pepper, transfer to a board and rest, covered, for 3 minutes.

To serve: Place the eggplants (aubergines) on plates, and fan the lamb over the vegetables.

NAVARIN OF LAMB

Navarin d'Agneau

1 boned leg of lamb
*   about 2 kg (4 lb)*
45 g (3 tablespoons) butter
1 large onion, diced
500 mL (2 cups) white wine
500 mL (2 cups) chicken stock
Bouquet garni: 3 sprigs parsley,
*   2 sprigs thyme and 2 bay leaves*
4 cloves garlic, crushed
Salt
Pepper
10 g (2 teaspoons) sugar

THE GARNISH
500 g (1 lb) baby carrots
6 turnips or 16 baby turnips
1 bunch small radishes
250 g (½ lb) pickling onions or
*   shallots*
4 asparagus stalks per person
2–3 tablespoons finely chopped
*   parsley*

Serves 6

THE *NAVARIN* IS a classic dish combining spring lamb with *primeurs*, the first vegetables of spring. Unlike the typical casserole, the *navarin* has no flour and is served unthickened as a light change-of-season stew. The combination of vegetables varies depending on the best available in the market.

Dice the lamb in 3 cm (1 in) cubes. Melt the butter in a large deep frying pan or a casserole, and brown the meat, one layer at a time. When the meat is well browned, add the onion and fry until translucent. Add the wine, stock and bouquet garni. Bring to the boil, reduce the heat and simmer for 15 minutes with the lid off. Add the garlic, season with salt and pepper, and continue to simmer with the lid on for a further 30 minutes.

After this time, add all the garnish vegetables except the asparagus. Simmer for a further 40 minutes, adding the asparagus 10 minutes before the end of cooking time.

To serve: With a slotted spoon, remove the meat and vegetables and place on a serving dish; keep warm. Reduce the liquid to sauce consistency, correct the seasoning, adding a little sugar to enhance the sweet spring vegetables, and spoon over the meat. Garnish with the parsley.

ROAST LAMB WITH WARM LENTIL SALAD

Agneau de Lait Rôti à la Salade Tiède de Lentilles

THE LENTILS
*250–300 g (8–9½ oz) dried brown
   or green lentils
45 mL (3 tablespoons) olive oil
1 small onion, diced (brunoise)
1 small carrot, diced (brunoise)
1 clove garlic, very finely chopped
2 tomatoes, peeled and chopped
500 mL (2 cups) chicken or veal stock
Salt
Pepper
15 mL (1 tablespoon) tomato paste
2 teaspoons thyme leaves*

THE LAMB
*1 baby leg, about 1.25 kg (2½ lb)
   plus 2 x 6-chop racks of lamb
Salt
Olive oil
1 sprig fresh rosemary
2 teaspoons wild thyme or savory
2 cloves garlic, cut in slivers*

THE JUS
*300 mL (1⅓ cups) lamb or veal
   stock
Salt
Pepper
Scant teaspoon tomato paste*

*30 mL (2 tablespoons) olive oil
30 rocket leaves (arugula)*

Serves 6

NOT A CLASSIC presentation, but one in the style of the younger chefs of Provence, who love to highlight traditional produce in unusual ways.

The lentils: An hour before needed, pour hot water over the lentils and allow to swell. Drain off the excess just before using. Heat the oil and toss the onion, carrot and garlic briefly. Add the lentils, stir once or twice to oil them, then add the tomatoes and stock. Season with salt, pepper, the tomato paste and thyme. Bring to the boil, reduce heat to a simmer, partially cover and cook for 25–30 minutes. By the time the lentils are softened (but not mushy), the liquid should be all but evaporated. Set aside.

The lamb: Rub the leg and racks (crown roasts) with salt and olive oil. Break up the rosemary into tiny pieces and press onto the meat, then pat on the thyme or savory. Stud the leg only with the garlic. Allow to sit for 1 hour before cooking.

When the lamb is ready for cooking, heat a film of olive oil in a heavy frying pan that can go in an oven and pan-fry the leg of lamb to a good colour on the outside, then do the racks. Remove the racks (crown roasts), return the leg and place the leg in the oven at 220°C (425°F, Gas 7) for 30–35 minutes, adding the racks (crown roasts) for the last 8 minutes. Remove the meat from the oven to a board, cover and rest for a further 8 minutes, while making the jus.

The jus: Deglaze the pan with some lamb or veal stock and the tomato paste. Stir to a light jus, then season to taste with salt and pepper.

To serve: Add 30 mL (2 tablespoons) olive oil to the lightly reheated lentils, stir and make a bed of these on each plate. Dot with rocket (arugula) leaves. Carve the lamb and on each bed of lentils lay three slices of leg roast, and 2 of the rack chops per person. Spoon about 30 mL (2 tablespoons) jus per person over each plate. Serve immediately.

MARINATED BARBECUED STEAK WITH ROASTED CAPSICUMS (SWEET PEPPERS)

Entrecôte Mariné aux Poivrons Rôtis

*6 porterhouse steaks, weighing
    about 200 g (6½ oz) each, or
    your favourite tender steak*
60 mL (4 tablespoons) olive oil
45 mL (3 tablespoons) red wine
1 teaspoon thyme leaves
2 red capsicums (sweet peppers)
2 yellow capsicums (sweet peppers)
2 green capsicums (sweet peppers)
Salt
Black pepper

Serves 6

HOW DO YOU make one steak look and taste different from another? Try this. Ideal for cooking on a barbecue, iron griddle or in a pan, it tastes just as good as it looks.

The steaks: Place the steaks in a large dish. Mix the oil and wine in a cup and pour over, then sprinkle with the thyme leaves. Leave for 1 hour minimum, turning at least once.

The capsicums (sweet peppers): Core and cut lengthways into the natural segments and with a small knife remove the seeds and pith. Lay skin-side up on a foil-lined baking sheet and place under a hot griller (broiler) until the capsicums (sweet peppers) blister and turn black. Do not shut the oven door or the flesh softens and cooks. When roasted, peel off the skin and set the vegetables aside. They may be kept in the fridge up to 2 days. If so, they will exude a natural oil in which they may be cooked; otherwise rub with olive oil.

To cook: On a barbecue or an iron griddle, cook the steaks when the grill is well heated. Always cook a little more on the first side than on the second. When the first side is half-cooked, turn the steaks at a 45° angle to create the typical grid mark of the barbecue or griddle. Season with salt and freshly ground black pepper only when turned over. When the steaks are ready to remove, toss the capsicums (sweet peppers) on the grill to reheat and pick up the grill marks. Serve, placed decoratively over the steaks.

PORTERHOUSE STEAK WITH ROASTED SHALLOTS AND OLIVE BUTTER

Entrecôte au Beurre d'Olives et aux Echalotes Rôties

THE OLIVE BUTTER
*125 g (8 tablespoons) butter,
preferably unsalted
2 tablespoons chopped shallots
About 8 pitted black olives
(depending on size), chopped
About 8 pitted green olives
(depending on size), chopped
Salt
Pepper
Dijon-style mustard to taste
Lemon juice to taste*

THE ROASTED SHALLOTS
*18 shallots or yellow or red pickling
onions
100 mL (⅓ cup) olive oil*

THE STEAKS
*Oil for the grill
3 double-thickness porterhouse
steaks
Salt
Pepper*

Serves 6

ONE OF THE NICEST ways to eat porterhouse steak (*entrecôte*), is to have the butcher cut it double thickness so that it can be crisply browned on the outside without losing the rare colouring inside. The meat is then carved for two servings. If eating rare meat is not for you, use the standard thickness of steak and serve one per person.

The olive butter: In a bowl, soften the butter with a whisk, then stir in the shallots, and black and green olives. Add the salt, pepper, mustard and lemon juice.

The roasted shallots: Rub the shallots or pickling onions with oil and place on a baking tray. Bake in the oven at 160°C (320°F, Gas 3) for 30–40 minutes, or until tender when pierced with a skewer.

To cook the steaks: Steaks of this thickness are at their best on a long iron grill or a cast-iron rangetop griddle, such as made by Le Creuset, although frying is possible. Heat the iron grill until it radiates a good heat, then oil lightly. Too much oil negates the corrugations. Cook the steaks to a little more than half on the first side (about 6 minutes, depending on thickness). When halfway through cooking on this side, turn the steaks by 45°, to mark out the crisscross imprint. Cook for 4 minutes on the second side, then season and transfer to a board. Rest for 2 minutes before carving.

To serve: Slice the steaks, half a steak per person, slices fanned open slightly. Top generously with olive butter. Serve with the roasted shallots or pickling onions. To eat the shallots or pickling onions, hold the root end with your fork and, using your knife, press the softened flesh from its peel.

TRADITIONAL BEEF DAUBE

Daube de Provence Traditionelle

1.5 kg (3 lb) beef shank or pot roast
250 g (½ lb) pork belly
Piece of fresh pork rind about
 10 x 6 cm (4 x 2½ in)
3 onions, chopped in wedges
5 cloves garlic, thinly sliced
3 medium carrots, thickly sliced
2-3 sprigs parsley
Piece orange peel
Stalk celery
Sprig thyme
2 bay leaves
12 peppercorns, lightly crushed
4 juniper berries, lightly crushed
Salt
Nutmeg
4 cloves
30 mL (2 tablespoons) wine
 vinegar
1 x 750 mL bottle (3 cups) red
 wine
50 g (3 tablespoons) lard or
 vegetable oil
30 mL (2 tablespoons) olive oil

Serves 6-8

PROBABLY THE BEST KNOWN Provençal dish, the *daube* is found with as many variations as there are cooks in Provence. Typical of them all is the long simmering of tender gelatinous cuts — not always beef, for there are *daubes* with lamb and pork — in a rich red wine sauce flavoured with strong root vegetables and the characteristic pieces of orange peel. This recipe may be varied by adding prunes or green or black olives in the last 30 minutes of cooking time.

Cut the beef and pork belly into large pieces; the rind in long strips. Set the pork pieces aside. Place the beef in a large dish with 1 onion, the garlic, carrots, parsley, orange peel, celery, thyme, bay leaves, peppercorns and juniper berries and spices. Add the wine vinegar and the red wine; set aside overnight to marinate. The next day, strain the ingredients, saving the marinade liquid, and then dry the meat and vegetables on paper towels.

In a large cast-iron casserole, heat the lard and colour the pieces of pork belly. Add the olive oil, the onion from the marinade and the beef and colour well. Add the pork rind and spread well through the meats, then pour on the reserved marinade liquid. Add the remaining onion wedges and the carrots and all the remaining spices and herbs of the marinade. Add enough water to cover the meat. Salt lightly, allowing for a lot of evaporation.

Bring to the boil, reduce the heat to the lightest simmer, skim once after 5 minutes, then cover with the lid. Cook slowly for 4-5 hours. Toward the end of the cooking time, remove the lid, reduce the sauce a little further if necessary, check seasonings when the juice is at desired sauce consistency and serve.

Most *daubes* are made in advance and benefit from reheating. When the *daube* is cold is the best possible time to degrease it, if you choose to do so, but the French of Provence often leave the fat to help oil the *macaronade* — the traditional pasta accompaniment, which may be large macaroni, penne, or noodles, tossed in butter, garlic and chopped parsley. It is also possible to sprinkle the top with a *persillade*, which is a mixture of finely chopped garlic and parsley.

BEEF DAUBE WITH BABY VEGETABLES

Daube de Provence Moderne

1.5 kg (3 lb) beef shank boned
OR 1-1.25 kg (2-2½ lb) beef
  shank still on the bone (ask the
  butcher to top and tail it, so it
  stands well, and to trim its flesh
  back at the thin end of the bone
  by about 5 cm [2 in]) plus 1 kg
  (2 lb) beef shank, cut in large
  slices
1 large onion, cut in 6 wedges
1 large carrot, diced
3 cloves garlic, finely chopped
2 bay leaves
3-4 sprigs fresh thyme
5 juniper berries, lightly crushed
10 peppercorns, lightly crushed
Piece orange peel
1 x 750 mL bottle (3 cups) red
  wine
60-75 mL (4-5 tablespoons) olive
  oil
2 tomatoes, peeled and roughly
  chopped
Salt
Pepper

THE GARNISH VEGETABLES
4 small globe artichokes, outer
  leaves removed, then quartered
  and 'choke' removed
6-8 Jerusalem artichokes (optional)
12-14 pickling onions
8-10 baby carrots

Serves 8

THOUGH THE METHOD of cooking this *daube* is similar to the preceding recipe, the result is remarkably more modern in presentation due to the cut of the beef shank and the unusual addition of baby vegetables.

Trim the outer fat or gristle off the beef portions. Lay the shin (if using) and the beef pieces in a large dish, cover with the onion, carrot, garlic, bay leaves, thyme, juniper berries, peppercorns, orange peel and wine. Leave overnight, turning occasionally.

The next day; strain the meat, keeping the liquid. Dry the meat, onion and carrot on paper towels, then heat the oil in a cast-iron casserole large enough to fit everything snugly, and brown the meat pieces first, followed by the onion and carrot. Add the reserved liquid, the rest of the marinade ingredients and the chopped tomato, then top up with water to just cover everything. Salt lightly, allowing for a lot of evaporation later.

Bring the dish to the boil, reduce the heat to the lightest simmer, skim once after 5 minutes, then cover with the lid and cook slowly for 4½ hours. Up to here there should be minimal evaporation.

Most *daubes* benefit from being made the day before they are to be eaten — this allows the flavours to consolidate. When the cooling is complete, store the *daube* overnight in the refrigerator; the grease will rise and set on the top. When the *daube* is to be eaten, lift off the layer of fat with a spoon, then reheat the meat. Meantime, cook the garnish vegetables in a pot of boiling salted water, starting with the globe artichokes, which take about 18-20 minutes, then adding the Jerusalem artichokes, if using (12-15 minutes), the baby carrots and pickling onions (8 minutes), so they finish cooking together.

To serve: Lift the meat out with a slotted spoon and keep warm, then bring the sauce up to a rolling boil and reduce by about half. Check the seasoning, add the garnish vegetables to the casserole to pick up the sauce, then arrange the meat pieces and vegetables decoratively on a large serving platter, with the beef on the bone (if using), forming the centrepiece. Serve with boiled, parsleyed potatoes, or, more traditionally, a *macaronade* (see *Daube de Provence Traditionelle*).

ROAST PORK WITH HERB STUFFING

Roulade de Porc aux Herbes

HERB STUFFING
*1 bunch spinach or silverbeet
    (Swiss chard)*
*3 sprigs thyme, leaves removed and
    finely chopped*
*2 sprigs rosemary, leaves removed
    and finely chopped*
*3 sprigs sage, leaves removed and
    finely chopped*
*½ bunch parsley, leaves removed
    and finely chopped*
Salt
Black pepper

*1 large boned jowl butt of pork,
    about 1.5 kg (3 lb)*
Salt
Pepper
*4 slices air-dried ham (or
    prosciutto)*
100 g (7 tablespoons) butter
1 carrot, diced
2 onions, diced
180 mL (¾ cup) water
1 clove garlic, finely chopped
1 bay leaf

Serves 8

A COMBINATION OF cooked spinach, air-dried ham and fresh herbs makes a great stuffing for this pork roast. The dish can be done with a shoulder of pork, but the jowl butt, a lesser known cut, is much easier to trim of fat and has larger amounts of gelatin to keep it succulent. Ask your butcher for it.

Devein the spinach or silverbeet (Swiss chard) and cook in boiling, salted water for about 3 minutes; refresh under cold water, drain and squeeze dry. Chop finely and put into a bowl. Add the finely chopped herbs to the spinach. Season with salt and freshly ground black pepper and mix well.

Starting from where the bone has been removed from the pork, cut a slit further into the eye of the meat with a sharp knife so that the meat can be opened out. Season the inside, then cover the surface with a layer of ham. Spread the herb stuffing over the ham, then roll the pork tightly and truss it along its length into a loaf shape.

Brown the meat in a heavy flameproof casserole. pour off excess fat, then add a little butter and sauté the carrot and onions until softened. Add the water, garlic and bay leaf. Cover, leaving the lid slightly ajar, and simmer slowly for 2 hours. When the meat is cooked, transfer it to a board, cover and rest for 10 minutes before cutting the strings and carving. Meantime, strain the sauce, checking it for salt and pepper.

To serve: Cut a few slices from the roll, place them on a serving dish, and surround with deep-fried *Panisses* (see page 118) or grilled slices of polenta.

PORK CASSEROLE WITH CAPERS

Ragoût de Porc aux Câpres

1.5 kg (3 lb) boned jowl butt of
   pork or pork shoulder (picnic
   shoulder)
200 g (7 oz) heavily smoked bacon
   (lard fumé), *cut into bite-sized
   pieces*
60 mL (4 tablespoons) olive oil
1 large onion, chopped
25 g (2 tablespoons) plain (all-
   purpose) flour
300 mL (1⅓ cups) dry white wine
   or light Rosé de Provence
300 mL (1⅓ cups) water
Bouquet garni: 1 small piece celery,
   1 sprig sage and thyme, 1 bay
   leaf, 3 stalks parsley
Salt
Pepper
2 tablespoons capers, rinsed well
1 tablespoon chopped imported
   gherkins (cornichons)

Serves 6

VINEGARED CAPERS ARE to be found along the Mediterranean, but the capers used in this recipe are dried and stored in salt. If you have difficulty finding them, ask for them in specialist Italian delicatessens. Rinse well before using.

Cut the meat into large cubes. Sauté the bacon in the base of a flameproof casserole, then, in the rendered fat plus the olive oil, sauté the pork pieces until well browned. Add the onion and brown to golden, then sprinkle in the flour and stir to the base of the pot. Add the wine and water, the bouquet garni and season lightly with salt and pepper. Bring to the boil, reduce the heat, cover and simmer for 1½ hours, or until tender.

When cooked, remove the meat to a bowl and keep it warm. Add the capers and chopped gherkins *(cornichons)* to the liquid in the casserole, reduce it to sauce consistency, check the seasoning and spoon the liquid over the meat. Serve with boiled potatoes, rice or boiled noodles with parsley.

BONED LOIN OF VEAL WITH TAPENADE

Carré de Veau à la Tapénade

1.5–2 kg (3–4 lb) boned loin of veal
35 g (2½ tablespoons) butter
Salt
Pepper
45 mL (3 tablespoons) water
1 recipe Tapénade (see page 142)
100 g (3½ oz) tuna canned in oil,
    drained and mashed
100 mL (⅓ cup) dry white wine

Serves 6

THE PUNGENT ANCHOVY and black olive combination of the classic *tapénade* is brought together here with tuna and used as a stuffing for veal in this unusual roast.

Tie the veal loin along its length with string to ensure it keeps a good shape during roasting. Place it in an oiled baking dish, spread the meat with 20 g (1½ tablespoons) butter, season with salt and pepper and roast in the oven at 220°C (425°F, Gas 7) for 1 hour. After 35 minutes, add the water to the dish to prevent any sediment burning. When the meat is cooked, transfer it to a board to rest for 10 minutes, covered with foil, then remove the string and slice the roast into thick 5 mm (¼ in) slices, without cutting right through.

Make up the *tapénade* recipe and add the mashed tuna. Spread a thick layer of this *tapénade* between each slice. Re-form the roast, holding it with two strings placed lengthways, if necessary. Return the meat to the baking dish and bake for a further 10 minutes at 200°C (400°F, Gas 6).

When cooked, transfer the meat to a serving platter, place the baking dish on the stove and deglaze the baking dish with the white wine. Bring to the boil, stir up any sediment in the base of the dish, blend well and boil to reduce the acidity of the wine. Check the seasoning, then add the remaining 15 g (1 tablespoon) butter before transferring the sauce to a sauceboat, to serve at the table with the sliced meat.

VEGETABLES

IF HERB-FLAVOURED vegetables simmered in olive oil, *beignets* (fritters) of zucchini flowers, and multi-vegetable minestrone-like soups are the main starters of a typical Provençal dinner, vegetables are rarely overlooked at later stages of the meal either.

Strangely, many of the vegetables we associate so keenly with the Mediterranean — tomatoes and capsicums (sweet peppers) particularly — were imports with the discovery of the New World, but one can scarcely imagine the cuisine of the area without them, so totally have they absorbed them as their own. On a checklist, tomatoes, capsicums (sweet peppers), eggplant (aubergine) and zucchini (courgettes) would top the local's list, but few outsiders recognise how typical also is silverbeet (Swiss chard) to the Comté of Nice, how familiar the small button squash (a summer squash), how delectable the baby peas, tiny green haricot beans and broad (fava) beans, how ubiquitous the violet-leaved globe artichoke and *topinambour* (Jerusalem artichoke), and how loved the asparagus.

Behind this love for vegetables is the peasant's almost symbiotic relationship with his land. Bar the city workers of the larger townships, up until recently, even those who did not work their own land had *potagers* (vegetable patches), and very often, as a gesture of social welfare, municipal councils provided small parcels of land outside the built-up areas for the poor to grow their own vegetables. Street markets abound, and in this sunny lifestyle where walking is a pleasure and a market visit a social outing, most people buy their vegetables fresh from stalls not supermarkets, providing a direct social link between the grower and the consumer, with time to discuss the merits of this plant, the drawbacks of another . . . and of course a recipe or two to cook it to its advantage. Time is not of the essence in countryside Provence.

Though simplicity reigns in so much of the cooking of the south, the Provençaux cook their vegetables with sophistication. Steaming or boiling is much too plain, and the characteristic approach is waterless cooking with the vegetable tossed in olive oil with herbs and garlic, or better still, olive oil, garlic (or onion) and tomatoes. Many vegetables are cooked in combination — the celebrated *ratatouille* is an example, but also the multi-layered *tian*, the gratins, the ragouts of multiple vegetables and the classic *artichauts à la Barigoule*, which at its simplest is a ragout of quartered artichokes with aromatic vegetables, and at its most sophisticated is a whole artichoke with a vegetable and meat stuffing.

Above all, if we learn anything as onlookers, my belief is that the lesson is twofold. First, buy only vegetables of the finest quality, and buy them regularly. They must be at their freshest, absolutely never bought for the week and held in a refrigerator. Secondly, there is this indomitable belief in France that smaller is better — a lesson so important one would wish to imprint it on the brains of all the greengrocers and growers of the English-speaking countries, with their hideous leanings toward only the large, polished, unblemished (should I say sterile?) and picture-postcard pretty.

In this field, the Provençaux know just how to profit from nature's bounty.

RATATOUILLE

Ratatouille

About 125 mL (½ cup) olive oil
2 onions, diced
1 large eggplant (aubergine),
   unpeeled and diced
3 large or 4 small zucchini
   (courgettes), unpeeled and diced
1 green capsicum (sweet pepper),
   sliced
2–3 cloves garlic, to taste, finely
   chopped
5 large ripe tomatoes, peeled,
   seeded and roughly chopped
Salt
Pepper
Tomato paste

Serves 6

COINED FROM THIS vegetable dish of southern France, the word 'ratatouille', meaning tossed or tumbled together, has gone into the French language to mean to get oneself into a mess. *Quelle ratatouille* . . . what a mess!

Heat 75–90 mL (⅓ cup) oil in a large frying pan. Sauté the onions until softened, then the cubes of eggplant (aubergine) and zucchini (courgettes). These last two should brown slightly. If the eggplant (aubergine) blots up the oil, add a little more when necessary. Stir in the capsicum (sweet pepper), garlic, and tomatoes. Cover and simmer gently for 15 minutes. Remove the lid and cook rapidly for another 2–3 minutes to remove the excess water. Season with salt, pepper and tomato paste.

Most often served hot in Provence, ratatouille is also delicious served cold with cold meats. When served cold, a little olive oil stirred through it gives a better texture.

TIAN OF VEGETABLES

Tian de Légumes

THE SILVERBEET (SWISS CHARD)
  LAYER
45 mL (3 tablespoons) olive oil
1 bunch silverbeet (Swiss chard),
  base of stalks removed, washed
  thoroughly, and coarsely
  shredded
15 g (1 tablespoon) pine nuts
Salt
Pepper
Nutmeg

THE TOMATO LAYER
45 mL (3 tablespoons) olive oil
1 small onion, chopped
1 clove garlic, finely chopped
1.25 kg (2½ lb) ripe tomatoes,
  peeled and roughly chopped
1 teaspoon fresh thyme or oregano
  leaves, the latter shredded
Salt
Pepper
Pinch sugar

THE EGGPLANT (AUBERGINE)
  LAYER
About 125 mL (½ cup) olive oil for
  frying
3 small eggplants (aubergines),
  unpeeled and sliced
Salt
Pepper
75 g (²/₃ cup) grated Mozzarella or
  Parmesan cheese
30 g (2 tablespoons) butter

'TIAN' IS THE NAME for a glazed earthenware dish, used for baking and gratinéeing, in which the locals cook this typical layered dish of vegetables. Now *tian* has become the name of the vegetable recipe itself. Some cooks go to great trouble to make their layering sophisticated and symmetrically patterned. This more rustic *tian*, of eggplant (aubergine), silverbeet (Swiss chard) and tomato is in the old style, and uses pre-cooked vegetables.

The silverbeet (Swiss chard) layer: Heat the olive oil in a frying pan and sauté the silverbeet (Swiss chard) until it softens. Add the pine nuts, stir and season with salt, pepper and nutmeg. Transfer to a rectangular ovenproof dish of about 20 x 25 cm (8 x 10 in).

The tomato layer: Heat the olive oil in a saucepan and sauté the onion until softened. Add the garlic, tomatoes, and thyme or oregano. Season with salt, pepper and sugar, then cook, stirring occasionally, for about 10 minutes, or until the mixture softens into a chunky sauce. Transfer to the ovenproof dish to make a layer over the silverbeet (Swiss chard).

The eggplant (aubergine) layer: Heat the oil in a frying pan and sauté the eggplants (aubergines), in batches if necessary, until lightly golden and softened. Season with salt and pepper. Drain slices on paper towels, then transfer to the dish as a top layer.

Top with the grated cheese, dot with a few knobs of butter and place it in the oven at 220°C (425°F, Gas 7) until reheated (20–30 minutes) and the cheese on top is melted and browned. You may wish to place it under a griller (broiler) for a moment to help crisp the cheese.

Fanned Eggplant (Aubergine) with Tomato and Capers

Aubergines en Eventail

90 mL (⅓ cup) olive oil
3 large onions, sliced
3 large eggplants (aubergines), not
  too fat
3 ripe tomatoes, thinly sliced
1 clove garlic, finely chopped
1 teaspoon fresh thyme leaves
2 tablespoons chopped parsley
1 tablespoon salt-packed capers,
  rinsed and drained
100 g (3½ oz) small black olives
Salt
Pepper
Optional: 50 g (⅓ cup) grated
  Gruyère (Swiss) cheese

Serves 4

THIS STRONGLY FLAVOURED VEGETABLE dish is suitable to accompany dark meats only. For vegetable lovers, the dish has enough character to stand alone as an appetiser.

Heat 60 mL (4 tablespoons) olive oil in a saucepan and slowly cook the onions until softened. Stir them well, then place a lid on the saucepan until they cook through (about 15–18 minutes).

Wash the eggplants (aubergines), but do not peel. With a stainless steel knife, cut off the stalk and slice 4–5 times (depending on width) lengthways to about 2 cm (¾ in) from the thinner stalk end. Fan out the segments and place a slice of tomato and a little garlic and a thyme leaf between each segment.

When the onions are ready, stir into them a further teaspoon thyme leaves and 1 tablespoon chopped parsley, and the capers and olives. Spread in the base of an ovenproof dish large enough to contain the eggplants (aubergine). Arrange the eggplant (aubergine) fans over the onion, drizzle with the remaining oil and season everything with salt and pepper. Cover the baking dish with aluminium foil and bake in the oven at 160°C (320°F, Gas 3) for 50 minutes, or until tender. Optional: Remove the foil, top with the grated cheese and return to the oven until the cheese melts.

Serve as a vegetable accompaniment to a meat dish, or on its own as an appetiser. It may be served with a tomato sauce (see Zucchini Flowers Stuffed with Mushrooms), or a sauce made from a seasoned purée of roasted capsicums (sweet peppers) (see Ravioli with Goat Cheese and Capsicum Cream Sauce).

EGGPLANT (AUBERGINE) CROWN

Couronne d'Aubergines

THE SAUCE
90-125 mL (¹⁄₃-½ cup) olive oil
1 onion, diced
4 large tomatoes, peeled and
  chopped
2 cloves garlic, finely chopped
Salt
Black pepper
Large sprigs oregano or marjoram

THE CROWN AND STUFFING
4 large eggplants (aubergines)
Olive oil for frying
Salt
Pepper
Chopped parsley
8 black olives, pitted and chopped
15 g (1 heaped tablespoon) pine
  nuts, roasted
2 cups cooked short-grain rice
20 g (2 tablespoons) grated
  Parmesan cheese

Serves 8

A PRETTY PRESENTATION from a ring mould lined with eggplants (aubergines) and stuffed with rice, black olives and pine nuts. Be sure to sauce the recipe only if it will not clash with the sauce of the dish it accompanies.

The sauce: Heat 45 mL (3 tablespoons) olive oil and sauté the onion until golden. Add the tomatoes, garlic, salt, pepper and a large sprig of oregano or marjoram. Simmer gently for 40 minutes; set aside.

The crown and stuffing: Slice 2 unpeeled eggplants (aubergines) lengthways in fine slices. Cut the rest into small dice. Heat about 45 mL (3 tablespoons) olive oil in a frying pan and sauté the sliced eggplants (aubergines) on both sides until golden; drain on paper towels. Add more oil if necessary and sauté the diced eggplants (aubergines), then add salt, pepper, parsley, olives and pine nuts. Cook for a further 5 minutes, mix in the rice, remove from the stove and stir in the Parmesan.

To assemble the crown: Line a 20–22 cm (8–9 in) ring mould with the slices of eggplant (aubergine). Overlap them slightly so that the filling cannot leak out. Fill the centre with the rice stuffing. Fold back the overhanging ends of the slices to hold the stuffing in position. Press slightly to insure everything is in place, then bake in the oven at 160°C (320°F, Gas 3) for 20 minutes. When cooked invert onto a serving plate. Serve with the reheated tomato sauce.

Note: If the crown is to be reheated, do not unmould it. Once the mould is removed, the crown swells and cannot be returned to the dish. The crown heats better in the steamy environment, rather than baking dry.

ARTICHOKE MEETS ARTICHOKE

Panaché d'Artichauts et Topinambours

3 globe artichokes
Lemon juice
Salt
6 Jerusalem artichokes
  (sunchokes), peeled and sliced
30 mL (2 tablespoons) olive oil
Chopped parsley
Black pepper

Serves 6–8

THIS UNIQUE DISH combines globe and Jerusalem artichokes for a wonderful contrast in textures.

The globe artichokes: Trim any wilted or discoloured leaves from the base of each artichoke, then cut the stem about 5 cm (2 in) from the base. Remove the outer leaves from the artichoke and cut off the top half of the globe (the fibrous part of the leaves). Cut the artichokes into quarters, remove the 'choke' (hairy centre) and rub well with lemon juice to prevent discolouration. Drop them into boiling, salted water and boil until tender, usually about 20–30 minutes.

The Jerusalem artichokes: Cook in a separate saucepan of boiling water until tender, 12–15 minutes.

To serve: Drain the artichokes well. Combine them, add the olive oil, parsley and freshly ground black pepper and toss well without reheating, then transfer to serving plates.

Variation: When Jerusalem artichokes are not in season, try making this dish with boiled and peeled broad (fava) beans tossed in the oil with the globe artichokes.

ARTICHOKES A LA BARIGOULE

Artichauts à la Barigoule

6 medium-to-large globe artichokes
Juice 2 lemons
250 g (½ lb) heavily smoked bacon
    (lard fumé), *cut into bite-sized*
    pieces
30 mL (2 tablespoons) olive oil
1 large onion, chopped
2 carrots, chopped
75 g (2½ oz) cultivated button
    mushrooms, sliced
100 mL (⅓ cup) white wine
2 small or 1 large clove garlic,
    finely chopped
Salt
Pepper
Chopped parsley for garnish

Serves 6

ONE OF THE CLASSIC vegetable dishes of Provence. The name comes from the Latin word for the sanguine mushrooms that were traditionally used in this dish, although it is more common now to see the ubiquitous *champignons de Paris* in their place. Alternatively, some say the name refers to the original serving method where the artichokes were cut low on their stems and trimmed of their tops, much like the shape of a mushroom. Nowadays the dish may be found with trimmed and quartered artichokes, as here, with artichoke bases attached only to their stems but with the leaves removed, or cooked whole, with the vegetable and ham inside as a stuffing. See if you like it this way . . .

Trim the outer leaves, then cut into four pieces, six if very large. Rub with lemon juice and leave each in acidulated water while trimming the rest.

Fry the bacon pieces in a frying pan without fat, both to render it and to crisp it. Remove, and in the rendered fat, to which you add a little olive oil if needed, sauté the onion until softened. Stir in the carrots and mushrooms, adding a little more olive oil, then place the artichoke pieces in the pan. Top with the white wine and garlic, salt and pepper.

Cover and simmer for about 30–40 minutes, or until the artichokes are tender. Remove the artichokes with a slotted spoon. If the sauce is too liquid, reduce it a little before finally checking the seasoning. Return the artichokes and spoon through the sauce, then serve topped with chopped parsley. Serve as a vegetable or as an appetiser.

BAKED FENNEL

Fenouils au Four

6 bulbs fennel (anise)
Salt
20 small pickling onions
2 carrots, sliced
4 tomatoes, peeled, seeded and
    roughly chopped
Pepper
45 mL (3 tablespoons) olive oil
1 bay leaf
½ teaspoon fresh thyme leaves
Chopped parsley for garnish

Serves 6

FENNEL IS AN aniseed-flavoured vegetable that is not used as widely as it should be. This typical recipe from the Marseilles area should convince the sceptics.

Trim the fennel bulbs and wash them. Blanch them in boiling, salted water for 10 minutes; drain. Halve them horizontally and place in a greased ovenproof dish. Scatter the bulbs with the onions, carrots and tomatoes. Season with salt and pepper, drizzle with the olive oil and add the bay leaf and thyme. Cover the dish with aluminium foil and bake in the oven at 200°C (400°F, Gas 6) for 1 hour. Serve garnished with parsley.

PROVENCAL PEAS

Petits Pois, Façon Du Coin

60 mL (4 tablespoons) olive oil
½ small onion, sliced or 10 whole
*   baby pickling onions or shallots*
350 g (11 oz) shelled green peas
1 large tomato, peeled and chopped
Salt
Pepper
Pinch sugar (optional, and only
*   when not using garlic)*

Serves 6

IF THE PROVENÇAUX seem to cook everything with garlic and tomato, maybe it's because they do. When you taste the flavour in this lovely pea recipe, you'll agree that perhaps they are right. If using sweet new season baby peas, the garlic is best omitted, but if you choose to substitute green beans or baby leeks for the peas, you'll find garlic a welcome addition.

Heat the olive oil in a saucepan or frying pan with some depth, choosing one with a well-fitting lid. Sauté the sliced onion until softened, or the whole pickling onions or shallots until shiny with oil. Add the peas and stir until they too are shiny, then add the tomato, salt, pepper and sugar. Cover with the lid, reduce the heat and simmer for 20–25 minutes (18–20 for very tender baby peas), stirring occasionally.

Variation: Both green beans and baby leeks suit this recipe beautifully. In both cases, add only the sliced onion, tomatoes and 2 cloves garlic, finely chopped. Omit the sugar, cook the beans for about 15–18 minutes, and the leeks until tender (depends on size).

POTATOES SAUTEED WITH GARLIC AND ROSEMARY

Pommes de Terre aux Gousses d'Ail et au Romarin

*5 large potatoes, peeled and diced
    (make them about 2 cm (1 in)
    square, but not too even)*
Olive oil for frying
*12-14 small whole cloves garlic,
    unpeeled*
*2 scant teaspoons fresh rosemary
    leaves*
Salt
Black pepper

Serves 6

THESE SAUTEED POTATOES are as tempting a potato dish as any I know.

Blanch the cut potatoes in a large saucepan of boiling, salted water for 4–5 minutes; drain and pat dry.

In a large frying pan, heat enough olive oil to cover the base of the pan and fry the potatoes. Allow to colour and crisp a little on one side before turning — too frequent turning prevents a good crisp fry. Add the garlic cloves and sauté with the potatoes, but watch they do not catch and colour too much on the base of the pan. Stir in the rosemary when the potatoes look about halfway to being golden and crisped. Turn frequently to ensure even browning. Add olive oil as necessary. Season with salt and pepper before serving.

POTATOES BRAISED IN SAFFRON STOCK

Pommes de Terre au Saffron

1 level teaspoon saffron threads
Pinch powdered saffron
1 L (4 cups) chicken stock
2-3 peeled and 'turned'
    (attractively shaped) oval
    potato pieces per person
Pepper

Serves 6-8

AN EXPENSIVE SPICE, saffron is well loved by the people of southern France. This recipe marries well with many of the fish dishes that the Provençaux cook with black olives and tomatoes.

Place the saffron and the boiling chicken stock in a small enamelled cast-iron casserole, and infuse to a strong orange colour. Simmer the potato pieces in this liquid very slowly in a 160°C (320°F, Gas 3) oven about 45 minutes, or until tender. Season with pepper.

STUFFED CABBAGE

Chou Fassum

1 green cabbage
Beef stock

THE STUFFING
500 g (1 lb) silverbeet (Swiss
    chard)
250 g (½ lb) heavily smoked bacon
    (lard fumé), diced
45 mL (3 tablespoons) olive oil
3 onions, chopped
100 g (3½ oz) pork rind, chopped
3 tomatoes, peeled and diced
2 cloves garlic, finely chopped
150 g (1 cup) long-grain rice,
    cooked, and drained if necessary
750 g (1½ lb) medium-grind
    sausage meat (ask your butcher
    for one that is seasoned but
    without bread)
Salt
Pepper

Serves 8

SOMETIMES KNOWN SIMPLY as *Fassum*, this stuffed cabbage dish from Grasse is a traditional grandmother's favourite. Few who have tasted such great rustic classics fail to appreciate the depth of flavour and the wonderful warm feeling of hearth and home that is conjured up by this style of cookery. Long may it reign!

The cabbage: Trim the stalk of the cabbage and remove any wilted or damaged outer leaves. Blanch the cabbage in boiling, salted water for approximately 15 minutes, refresh under cold water to help retain its colour, then drain upside down in a colander until fully cool. Squeeze gently between the palms to expel excess water.

The stuffing: Blanch the silverbeet (Swiss chard) in boiling, salted water for 5 minutes, refresh under cold water and drain, squeezing to expel as much moisture as possible. Chop, then place in a bowl. Crisp the bacon in a small frying pan spread with a minimal amount of oil. Add to the bowl, then add a little more oil to the pan and sauté the onions until translucent. Add to the bowl. Blanch the pork rind for 2 minutes, then add it to the bowl with the tomatoes and garlic. Gently spread the cabbage leaves open and remove the heart of the cabbage. Chop the heart and add it to the bowl. Finally, fold in the rice and the raw sausage meat, and season with salt and pepper.

To stuff and cook the cabbage: Spread the leaves of the cabbage and insert the stuffing between them as evenly as possible, making a medium-sized layer in the centre to replace the cabbage heart. Push the leaves into place around this 'heart', using the stuffing between the leaves to hold the cabbage shape in place. Some housewives string the cabbage, suggesting that it is easier to remove from the cooking pot later, but you may find that string pulls through the flesh of the cabbage when it is cooked and tender, so instead simply press the cabbage into shape with the palms of the hand and transfer it, core-side down, into a large saucepan in which it fits snugly.

Cover the cabbage with stock. Bring to the boil, reduce the heat, cover the saucepan and simmer gently for 3½ hours. To remove from the saucepan, lift gently with two slotted spoons angled from each side (if you have a helper, three spoons are even better!) and transfer to a plate.

To serve: These rustic dishes should be presented simply in a large shallow bowl with a few ladles of the broth spooned around, and some in a sauceboat to serve at the table. Any leftover broth is served as soup, or used as a soup base the next day, and the wonderfully perfumed stuffed cabbage is cut into wedges and served at winter dinners accompanied only by boiled potatoes and the mustard pot.

CHICKPEA FRITTERS

Panisses

250 g (½ lb) chickpea (garbanzo
    bean) flour
1 L (4 cups) cold water
Salt
Light olive oil or grape seed oil for
    frying
Pepper

CHICKPEAS ARE A favourite ingredient of the Provençaux. They are most well known for being the essential ingredient in *socca*, a chickpea-flour pancake which is cooked on special hotplates. Here chickpea flour is made into fritters called *panisses*, which can be served as an appetiser with a small *mesclun* (mixed green) salad. From time to time they are used as a vegetable to accompany a *daube* or a roast.

Pour the chickpea flour into a saucepan and, stirring all the time, add the cold water. Bring slowly to the boil, adding salt to taste. Cook for about 8 minutes, stirring continually to prevent lumps. Cover your hands, as the mixture spatters as it boils. Pour it into a shallow dish, preferably square or rectangular, filling to a depth of about 1 cm (½ in). When cool (this can be done the day before) unmould and cut into strips of around 2 cm (¾ in) wide and 8 cm (3½ in) long.

Heat the oil in a deep fryer to about 160°C (320°F). Deep-fry the *panisses* until golden, then transfer to a tray lined with paper towels to drain off excess oil. Season with salt and pepper.

MARINATED PRESERVED VEGETABLES

Légumes à l'Huile

THE MARINADE
30 mL (2 tablespoons) olive oil
1 large onion, finely chopped
1 small carrot, finely chopped
4 cloves garlic
500 mL (2 cups) white wine
vinegar
500 mL (2 cups) water
1 large sprig thyme
1 large sprig rosemary
1 large sprig marjoram
15 whole peppercorns
1 kg (2 lb) button mushrooms, as
white as possible
or 4 medium eggplants
(aubergines), unpeeled and
thinly sliced through their
length
or 1 kg (2 lb) assorted coloured
capsicums (sweet peppers),
seeded and cut into natural
segments
or 1 kg (2 lb) baby artichokes,
with 2.5-4 cm (1-1½ in) stalks,
the bulb part pared and
trimmed to tender part only
Olive oil to cover vegetables (about
1 L [4 cups])

KEEPING THE CROP and prolonging the seasons has always been a challenge for cooks. French southerners do this with traditional flavours of the region — olive oil and herbs. These preserved vegetables are served with cold meats or as part of an hors d'oeuvre.

The marinade: Put a film of olive oil in a saucepan large enough to contain the vegetables easily. Heat, and when warm but not hot enough to sizzle, add the chopped onion and carrot and fry slowly until they soften. Add the garlic, vinegar, water, herbs and peppercorns and boil for 10 minutes. Add the chosen vegetables to the hot liquid, remove the pan from the heat and allow to stand for 15 minutes. Drain and cool.

Pack in sterilised glass preserving jars and cover with olive oil. You may also add a few fresh sprigs thyme and a small bay leaf to each bottle. Seal the jars and stand for about 1 month in a cool place. The vegetables can be kept for several months providing they remain covered with olive oil. Be warned, if any part of the vegetable protrudes from the oil, it is capable of carrying air into its flesh and fermenting, and must be discarded. Kept well down and steeped in oil, they will last for months.

DESSERTS

WHEN THERE IS HONEY from the sweet-smelling, sun-soaked flowers on the hillsides, fruit on the trees, and the weather is too hot to do any tediously long cooking, it is little wonder that the Provençaux most often finish their meal with cheese or fruit.

A glance at old regional cookbooks may amaze sweet-toothed foreigners — most have no dessert chapter, and if anything sweet is indicated, it is more likely to be a series of recipes for fruit jams, instructions for domestic methods of candying fruit, recipes for small-scale confectionery (marzipans, jellies, simple fruit bonbons), or methods of preserving fruit for storage, including turning it into a variety of home-made liqueurs such as curaçao, anisette, walnut liqueurs and *ratafias* made from crushed fruit, filtered and blended with *eau-de-vie*. Household cupboards abound with preserving jars filled with *eau-de-vie*, whose buckle-down lids provide easy access for the addition of a few pieces of every type of fresh fruit as it comes into season.

A large basket of fresh fruit is a typical end of meal offering, and when not eaten raw, simple methods suffice to cook the fruits — slices of orange in syrup, or made into a sorbet, a compôte of apples with prunes, figs or pears poached in white wine, strawberries served with red wine and sugar, and maybe, on an ambitious day, a rustic apple tart.

Apricots, peaches, plums, figs, quinces, pears and apples . . . the region is so blessed with fruit trees, it almost single-handedly produces all the dessert and jam-making fruit of France. The fig tree is as visible as the olive tree, and perhaps the region's favourite fruit, but no less prized are the strawberries of Carpentras, the April joy of the sweet-smelling melons of Cavaillon, or the summer onset of the cherry harvest in the Gapeau valley and the countryside around Brignoles. Green and black grapes are grown for eating in the coastal area, which is also part of the citrus belt that lines the Mediterranean from Turkey to Spain. The wonderful bitter oranges of Nice, the tangerines of Antibes and the lesser-known, large, fleshy but almost juiceless citron, or *cédrat*, are plucked from the trees for the tiny confiseries (candy shops) of Apt, Oraison and Grasse. Here they produce some of the best quality *fruits confits* (candied fruit) in the world.

If the fresh fruit of the region is renowned — exported, eaten fresh, made into jams at Apt, Oraison and Robion — the dried fruit of the area is not to be overshadowed. The almond tree has so long grown on the slopes of the Alpes de Provence, most consider it as a native, and Digne and Aix-en-Provence have since medieval days

been the capitals of a thriving industry. Almonds dominate local confectionery
— they are mixed with honey to create the famous nougats of Montélimar,
the bite-sized iced almond paste pastels called *calissons d'Aix*, and the *dragées*
and *berlingots* of Carpentras and Aix. Walnuts abound, hazelnuts too, and pine
nuts have been grown on the coast since Roman days.

If there is no Christmas celebration without *les santons* (the traditional clay-
baked painted figurines that represent the nativity and are found in houses,
churches and exhibition halls over the festive season), then neither is there
Christmas without *le gros soupa* on Christmas Eve. This 'supper of the nativity' is
full of ritual. To symbolise the *Saint Trinité*, the table is laid with three candles
arranged on three tablecloths, each smaller than the one below it. Seven items
dress the table in the name of the seven Stations of the Cross — among them for
most people are garlic, sage, and usually a whole fish. At the end of the meal, but
sometimes set in elaborate decoration on a nearby sideboard, both fresh and dried
fruits play the champion role — the thirteen *mendiants*, representing Christ and
the Apostles. Imperative are dates, walnuts, hazelnuts, figs, grapes, almonds,
nougats (both white and black), dried black grapes (raisins or muscatels), melons,
citrus fruit, *confiseries* such as *calissons* or *dragées*, and local cakes. A large brioche
made with oil is common, but in Nice around Christmas time an egg-enriched,
sweetened version of the *fougasse*, the *fougassette*, is baked with orange peel and
cédrat, and flavoured with orange flower water. The most celebratory ones can be
almost trellis-like in shape.

FIGS POACHED IN WHITE WINE AND HONEY

Figues Pochées au Miel

500 mL (2 cups) fruity white wine
45 mL (3 tablespoons) honey
Juice 1 lemon
¼ teaspoon cinnamon
12 figs

Serves 6

THE FIG TREE is almost as common to the Provençal landscape as the olive tree. In this dish figs are combined with honey, traditionally produced all along the Mediterranean hillsides, but particularly in the foothills of the Alpes Maritimes, where lavender honey is especially prized. When figs are not in season, try the dish with peeled whole pears, cooked for about 20 minutes, or until tender.

In a saucepan combine the wine, honey, lemon juice and cinnamon. Bring to the boil. Add the figs, reduce the heat and simmer for 2–3 minutes, depending on the ripeness of the figs. Transfer the figs to a bowl. Reduce the liquid by boiling down to about 250 mL (1 cup). Pour over the figs. Refrigerate and serve cold, with or without cream, as preferred.

Figs Poached in Red Wine and Raspberries

Figues Pochées aux Framboises

500 g (1 lb) raspberries
400 g (1²/₃ cups) superfine sugar
750 mL (3 cups) red wine,
 preferably a light, soft red
18 figs
125 mL (½ cup) water
Peel of 1 orange, cut in julienne
 strips to decorate

Serves 6

WHEN THE LAST of the summer raspberries coincide with the first of the autumn figs, rush to the stove, for this is a dessert made in heaven.

Purée the raspberries in a food processor or blender and strain out the seeds. Place the purée in a saucepan with the 150 g (²/₃ cup) sugar. Bring to the boil and stir until the sugar dissolves; add the wine and return to the boil then reduce the heat to a simmer.

 Poach the figs in this mixture, uncovered, over a low heat for 5 minutes, turning them once. Remove the figs with a slotted spoon and place them in a shallow bowl. Reduce the sauce to about 300 mL (1¼ cups) and cool.

 Place the water and remaining sugar in a saucepan and bring to the boil, stirring so that the sugar is dissolved before the water boils. Add the orange peel and cook until it softens and has a glossy sheen (about 4 minutes). Drain.

 Serve the figs cold with the red wine and raspberry sauce. Decorate with the orange strips.

POACHED PEARS WITH FRESH BASIL

Poires Pochées au Basilic

8 pears, peeled but stems intact
1 lemon, halved
500 mL (3 cups) fruity white wine
45 mL (3 tablespoons) crème de
    cassis *(optional)*
100 g (3½ oz) sugar
1 vanilla bean, halved
200 mL (1 scant cup) water
10 basil leaves

Serves 8

POACHED FRUITS ARE a typical dessert of the south, but this version has an interesting twist. Try it also with peaches or nectarines, altering the poaching time until your chosen fruit is tender.

After peeling the pears, rub each one with lemon, to prevent discolouration.

Choose a casserole dish or saucepan large enough to fit the pears snugly and add the white wine, cassis (if using) and sugar. Bring to the boil, add the vanilla bean and then the pears. Top up with water, reduce the heat and simmer for about 20–25 minutes, depending on the ripeness of the pears. Without pricking the pears, turn them once if they are not fully submerged. When cooked, turn off the heat and throw in the basil leaves. Leave to cool in the liquid.

Just prior to dinner, remove the pears to a platter and reduce the syrup to about one-third of its volume, until it is thick and syrupy. Spoon the liquid and basil leaves over the pears just as you serve.

Variation: A modern touch would be to add 1 tablespoon green peppercorns, drained of their brine, to the syrup while poaching. The tang of the pepper is an interesting addition.

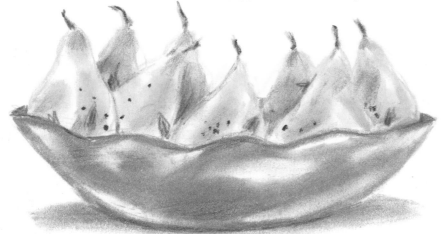

SUMMER BERRIES WITH MUSCAT DE BEAUMES-DE-VENISE

Fruits Rouges au Muscat de Beaumes-de-Venise

150 g (1 cup) strawberries
150 g (1 cup) raspberries
150 g (1 cup) blackberries
150 g (1 cup) blueberries
100 g (²/₃ cup) redcurrants
Grated peel of 1 orange (for texture, use the smallest julienne grater, not the nutmeg-style mesh of the grater)
30 g (2 tablespoons) sugar
150 mL (²/₃ cup) Muscat de Beaumes-de-Venise *or other fruity, sweet wine such as late-arrested Frontignac or Sauternes*

Serves 6

THE SUN-DRENCHED CLIMATE of Provence has made it a haven for fruits. Summer berries are often soused with red wine and sugar, but the beautiful sweet white dessert wine of Beaumes-de-Venise is one of the region's most renowned. If you are able to spoon the berries into a melon from Cavaillon, you'll have before you some of the finest elements in the world for a simple dessert.

Hull the strawberries and combine in a bowl with the other fruit. Add the grated peel, sprinkle with sugar and then pour over the *Muscat de Beaumes-de-Venise*. Leave to macerate for about 1 hour before eating.

FRESH FIG AND WALNUT TART

Tarte aux Figues et aux Noix

THE SHORTCRUST PASTRY
*200 g (1¾ cups) plain (all-purpose)
    flour*
*100 g (7 tablespoons) unsalted
    butter, softened*
1 egg yolk
*60 g (4 tablespoons) superfine
    sugar*
About 45 mL (3 tablespoons) water

THE FILLING
*75 g (5 tablespoons) unsalted
    butter, softened*
100 g (generous ⅓ cup) caster sugar
125 g (2 cups) ground walnuts
1 teaspoon arrowroot or cornstarch
*Few drops vanilla extract or pinch
    cinnamon*
2 egg yolks, or 1 whole egg

THE DECORATION
*About 15 small figs, preferably
    small, brown and pointed*
20 fresh walnut halves
Icing (confectioners') sugar

Serves 8

TWO MAJOR FRUITS of the hillsides of Provence come together in this very decorative tart.

The shortcrust pastry: Place the flour on a slab of marble or other cool surface. Make a well in the centre and add the butter, egg yolk, sugar and 30 mL (2 tablespoons) water. Mix the ingredients in the well together, then bit by bit incorporate the flour.

When there are no specks of white flour separate from the butter, add another 15 mL (1 tablespoon) water and continue to blend until the pastry forms a ball. Taking care not to knead too much lest you introduce too much elasticity, knead the dough with the heel of the hands until it becomes springy. Alternatively, blend together the pastry ingredients in a food processor. Then form into a ball, wrap in plastic wrap and leave for about 20 minutes (in refrigerator in hot weather) before rolling out and lining a 28 cm (11 in) tart mould.

The filling: Cream the butter and sugar until light and fluffy. Add the ground walnuts, arrowroot or cornstarch and vanilla or cinnamon, then stir in the egg yolks or whole egg. Spread into the pastry base. Arrange the decoration by halving the figs and placing them skin-side down in a spiral pattern over the top of the flan. Dot the walnut halves between the figs. Sprinkle with icing (confectioners') sugar and bake in the oven at 220°C (425°F, Gas 7) for 30–35 minutes, checking after 25 minutes that the figs are not caramelising too much. If they do, reduce heat back to 200°C (400°F, Gas 6) to finish the cooking. Serve slightly warm or at room temperature.

PINE NUT TART

Tarte aux Pignons

THE SHORTCRUST PASTRY
*250 g (2 cups) plain (all-purpose)
    flour*
*140 g (9 tablespoons) unsalted
    butter*
1 egg yolk
40 g (2 level tablespoons) sugar
*About 30-45 mL (2-3 tablespoons)
    water*

THE FILLING
*300 g (9½ oz) chopped imported
    candied fruit (orange, orange
    peel and cédrat)*
*45 mL (3 tablespoons) Grand
    Marnier liqueur*
Grated rind 1 orange
*150 g (10 tablespoons) very soft
    butter*
125 g (½ cup) superfine sugar
125 g (1¼ cups) ground almonds
3 eggs
*200 g (6½ oz) pine nuts or very
    coarsely chopped macadamia
    nuts*

Serves 10

WITH ALMONDS FROM Aix-en-Provence, the capital of almond production in France, pine nuts collected from the coastal pines since Roman days, and candied fruit from Apt, the world capital for artisanal quality glacéed fruit, no wonder these interesting ingredients come together in this unique tart.

Although you may use a broad variety of glacéed fruit, the tart flavours are at their best with a predominance of orange and lemon fruit and peel mixed with the less widely known *cédrat*, sometimes known as citron.

The shortcrust pastry: Make the pastry as in Fresh Fig and Walnut Tart (see page 126). Rest for 30 minutes. When ready, roll out and line a 26–28 cm (10–11 in) tart mould with the pastry.

The filling: Macerate the glacéed fruit with Grand Marnier and orange peel for a few hours or overnight.

In a bowl or food processor, cream the butter and sugar, then add the almonds and eggs, one at a time. Add the candied fruit and mix well. Spread over the pastry, then add the pine nuts or macadamia nuts and push down into the creamed mixture. Bake in the oven at 190°C (375°F, Gas 5) for 45 minutes. If the mixture browns too readily, reduce the heat to 180°C (350°F, Gas 4) for the last 10 minutes. Serve at room temperature not refrigerated.

APPLE AND SILVERBEET (SWISS CHARD) TART
Tourte aux Blettes

THE SHORTCRUST PASTRY
400 g (3 cups plus 2 tablespoons)
plain (all-purpose) flour
250 g (1 cup) unsalted butter
1 egg yolk
80 g (4 tablespoons) superfine
sugar
About 45 mL (3 tablespoons) water

THE FILLING
8 leaves silverbeet (Swiss chard),
stalks removed
100 g (½ cup) soft brown sugar
2 eggs
60 g (⅓ cup) sultanas (golden
raisins) macerated in 45 mL (3
tablespoons) dark rum
100 g (3½ oz) pine nuts
40 mL (3 tablespoons) Marc de
Provence *(may be replaced with*
brandy or Kirsch)
Pinch pepper
15 mL (1 tablespoon) light olive oil
3 Granny Smith apples, peeled,
cored and sliced
1 whole egg, beaten with a fork, for
glazing

Serves 8

FROM THE COMTÉ de Nice, where the love of silverbeet (Swiss chard) is so often reflected in the cookery, comes this unusual apple tart, locally known as *tourta de blèa*. A dessert to surprise you.

The shortcrust pastry: Using the ingredients in this list, make up a shortcrust pastry following the method of the Fresh Fig and Walnut Tart (see page 126). Rest the pastry for at least 30 minutes (it may be made the day before).

The filling: Wash the silverbeet (Swiss chard) thoroughly; dry and shred. Put the brown sugar in a bowl or food processor and mix in the eggs one at a time, stirring well to dissolve the sugar. Add the sultanas (golden raisins), drained of rum, the pine nuts, liqueur, pepper, and olive oil. Stir everything well and then add the silverbeet (Swiss chard).

To assemble the tart: Roll out half the pastry and line the base of a 28 cm (11 in) tart mould. Spread the filling into the base. Line the top of the filling with a layer of sliced apples, spiralled around the tart. Roll out the remaining pastry to the size of the top of the tart mould, and place this disc of pastry on top of the filling. Tuck the edges inside the pastry coming up from the base layer, and neaten the edges, cutting off any excess pastry.

Brush the top of the tart with the beaten egg as a glaze, and prick in a circular fashion with a fork. Bake in the oven at 200°C (400°F, Gas 6) for 45–50 minutes, or until cooked through and a rich brown on top. Although it is not traditional in Nice, this tart is lovely with whipped cream.

LEMON SOUFFLE

Soufflé au Citron

6 egg yolks
50 g (3 tablespoons) sugar
1 teaspoon grated lemon rind
100 mL (7 tablespoons) lemon juice
9 egg whites
100 g (7 tablespoons) extra sugar
Icing (confectioners') sugar for
    dusting

Serves 8

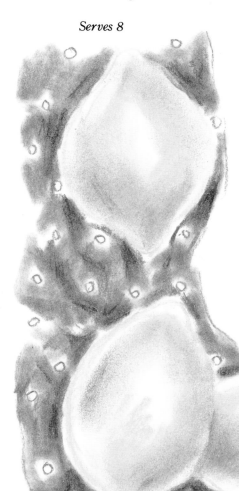

IF YOU LOVE the texture of hot soufflés with their blow-away lightness, but do not have a sweet tooth, this one is sure to become a favourite.

Put the egg yolks, sugar, rind and lemon juice into a bowl over a saucepan of hot water and whisk over heat until the mixture increases in volume and becomes mousse-like in consistency. The heat is to help the sugar soften, but the mixture must not become hot or the eggs will poach. The mixture should not rise above 75°C (167°F).

Remove the bowl and continue to beat until the mixture cools a little. Whisk the egg whites with the extra sugar until stiff and then fold gently through the mixture.

Pour the mixture into 8 small custard cups, buttered and sugared. With a metal spatula, carefully remove the excess soufflé mixture by sliding the spatula across the top of the bowls to level off the surface. Place in the oven at 180°C (350°F, Gas 4) and bake for 15 minutes. After 12 minutes of cooking time, quickly dust the soufflés with icing (confectioners') sugar and return to the oven for the final 3 minutes of cooking. The icing (confectioners') sugar caramelises, giving these light-coloured soufflés an appealing dark lid.

To serve: Place each soufflé on the side of a small dessert plate and place a scoop of ice cream of your choice on the side to serve with it.

CREME CARAMEL WITH GLAZED ORANGE

Crème Renversée aux Oranges Confites

THE CARAMEL
120 g (½ cup) sugar
135 mL (½ cup plus 1 tablespoon)
  water

THE CUSTARD
600 mL (2½ cups) milk
60 g (4 tablespoons) sugar
4 eggs

THE GLAZED ORANGES
600 g (2½ cups) sugar
1 L (4 cups) water
5 navel oranges

Serves 6

FOR THOSE WHO cannot buy the fabulous glacéed fruit candied in Apt and Carpentras, where whole fruit is steeped in sugar syrup for days and cooked until its glossy sheen has penetrated right to the centre, there is a quick method below for making your own. Here, a crème caramel is combined with a chewy, tangy base of glazed orange. *Vive la différence!*

The caramel: In a small saucepan, bring the sugar and water to the boil, stirring to make sure the sugar dissolves before the water boils, otherwise it may crystallise. Have ready a large bowl of water. When the caramel turns brown, place the base of the saucepan in the bowl to stop the caramel browning any further. When cooled enough not to damage them, pour a small layer of caramel into the base of 6 x 150 mL (1 cup) custard cups.

When ready to make the custard, place 2–3 slices of glazed orange (see below) in the base of each ramekin, depending on the volume available. If you prefer, chop them and add them diced.

The custard: Bring the milk to the boil with the sugar. Break the eggs into a bowl and whisk well. When the milk is hot, pour it onto the eggs, whisking continuously to blend them well. Strain and pour on top of the oranges in the ramekins. Place the ramekins in a baking dish of hot water, and bake in the oven at 190°C (375°F, Gas 5) for 20–25 minutes. Test by probing with a skewer; it should be hot, and bear no trace of milkiness. Cool and invert onto small plates to serve.

The glazed oranges: Heat the sugar in the water, stirring until it dissolves. Top and tail the oranges. Slice into approximately 5 mm (¼ in) slices. Allow the syrup to cool slightly. Place the slices in the base of a wide pan and cover with the syrup. Bring to a simmer, and cook for about 30 minutes, making sure the flesh does not disintegrate.

Remove the oranges to a 1 L (1 qt), sterilised glass preserving jar; reduce the syrup to about three-quarters its volume, then pour over the oranges, ensuring they are well covered with syrup (you may top up with a little water and shake the sealed jar). When cool, seal the jar. Do not use for at least 24 hours. Keeps for months.

Honey Bavarian Cream with Lavender Custard

Bavarois au Miel à la Crème à la Lavande

THE MERINGUE ITALIENNE
125 g (½ cup) sugar
100 mL (3½ fl oz) water
125 g (½ cup) egg white (4 large
  eggs)

THE BAVARIAN CREAM
50 g (2 tablespoons) honey,
  preferably an aromatic one or
  the true miel de Provence,
  which is made from lavender
  and herb flowers
2 scant teaspoons (1 envelope)
  gelatine
500 mL (2 cups) heavy cream

LAVENDER CUSTARD
500 mL (2 cups) milk
100 g (7 tablespoons) sugar
4 egg yolks
1 tablespoon fresh lavender flowers

Serves 8

SOMEWHAT TRICKY TO MAKE, this dessert is typical of the lighter style of the *nouvelle pâtisserie*. It is filled with the delicate aroma of the lavender-laden hillsides in the perfume-producing areas behind the Côte d'Azur. If you cannot obtain lavender honey, choose the most aromatic one you can find.

The meringue italienne: Combine the sugar and the water in a small saucepan and bring to the boil, stirring to make sure the sugar dissolves before the water boils. Whip the egg whites to firm peaks with an electric beater. When the sugar syrup reaches 118°C (244°F) on a sugar thermometer — or when the bubbles on the top of the saucepan are evenly distributed right across the top, and of even, fairly small size — remove from the heat and pour in a thin stream over the egg white, beating all the time until all the syrup is incorporated.

The Bavarian cream: In a saucepan, warm the honey and, when hot, add the gelatine (softened first in a little water to swell it). Stir until the gelatine disappears. Cool without setting, then add the honey and gelatine mixture to the meringue italienne, folding it in gently. Whip the cream to soft peaks only. When the base mixture is cool, gently fold the cream into it.

Place the circle, or the buckled-up walls of a 20 cm (8 in) springform tin without its base, onto a large serving platter. Pour the mixture into the mould and transfer it to the refrigerator for a minimum of 4 hours to set.

The lavender custard: Bring the milk to the boil in a saucepan. In a bowl, blend the sugar with the egg yolks. Pour on a little of the hot milk, stirring, then return the egg mixture to the saucepan and stir well with a whisk until the mixture thickens. It must not boil. Remove the saucepan from the stove, stir in about 1 tablespoon fresh lavender flowers, pour into a jug and leave overnight in the refrigerator. The next day, strain out the lavender through a fine sieve, return the custard to a jug, and cover with plastic wrap until needed.

To serve: Run a knife around the wall of the mould and lift off the circle. Serve either as a whole piece, with Lavender Custard poured around the border or alongside, or cut in wedges and place on individual plates on a pool of custard.

ROSEMARY SORBET

Sorbet au Romarin

125 mL (½ cup) water
125 g (½ cup) sugar
5 tablespoons fresh rosemary leaves
90 mL (⅓ cup) lemon juice
500 mL (2 cups) cold, dry white
   wine

Makes 1 L (4 cups)

THE WILD HERBS grown on the hillsides of Provence are used extensively in cooking, but for the most part show up in savoury dishes. This rosemary sorbet, made also with savory or wild thyme, highlights the herbs in a different guise . . . it may be served as a palate cleanser between successive courses in a heavy meal, it may be used as an apéritif on a hot day, or it may be served as a dessert.

The syrup: In a saucepan combine the water, sugar and rosemary leaves. Stir and bring to the boil. Simmer slowly for 5 minutes. Remove from the stove and when cool, refrigerate overnight.

   The next day, strain out the rosemary, take 60 mL (4 tablespoons) syrup, add the lemon juice and the cold wine. Use an ice cream machine, following the manufacturer's directions or freeze in a tray. If using the latter method, remove when partially frozen, stir well to break up the crystals and continue to freeze until set.

   If using as a palate cleanser, serve by spooning it into cold, stemmed glasses. As a dessert, it may be served alone or as a complement to fresh fruit, particularly berries.

ORANGE AND CITRON PARFAIT

Terrine Glacé au Cédrat et à l'Orange

100 g (7 tablespoons) sugar
75 mL (5 tablespoons) cold water
4 egg yolks
20 g (1½ tablespoons) crystallised
  ginger, chopped
20 g (1½ tablespoons) imported
  mixed candied peel, chopped
20 g (1½ tablespoons) angelique,
  chopped
20 g (3 tablespoons) pecan nuts,
  split in half
20 g (1½ tablespoons) pistachios
30 g (3 tablespons) cédrat (citron)
¼ teaspoon cinnamon
300 mL (1¼ cups) heavy cream,
  whipped
30 mL (2 tablespoons) Kirsch

Serves 6

AN ICED PARFAIT like the *Soufflé Glacé à l'Anis*; but this time it is presented in a terrine, so that it may be cut in slices. To complement the orange, the dessert is made with *citron* or *cédrat*, a thick-skinned citrus fruit, rather scarce on juice, but whose fleshy peel candies well. If you find it hard to obtain, try an Italian delicatessen, for Italians often serve *cédrat* with cheese platters.

Put the sugar in a saucepan with the cold water. Stir to ensure the sugar dissolves before the water boils. Boil down until it reaches the 'jelly' stage, 118°C (244°F) on a sugar thermometer. If you do not have a thermometer, look for even-sized small bubbles all the way across the top.

Lift the saucepan from the stove for 30 seconds, then pour the syrup in a stream onto the egg yolks in a large bowl, and whisk with an electric mixer until the mixture has cooled, when it will be whitish in colour, double its volume and nearly as thick as whipped cream. Fold in the chopped ginger, peel and angelique, the nuts, *cédrat* and cinnamon, followed by the whipped cream. Flavour with Kirsch.

Pour into a 1 L (1 qt) loaf tin or terrine and cover with plastic wrap. Leave for a minimum of 8 hours to set. It will keep for up to 4 days. Best served with a garnish of fresh orange segments or slices, preferably glazed.

ICED SOUFFLE WITH STAR ANISE AND PASTIS

Soufflé Glacé à l'Anis

230 g (1 cup) sugar
About 90-125 mL (⅓-½ cup)
   water
8 egg yolks
60 mL (4 tablespoons) Pernod,
   Ricard or other pastis
500 mL (2 cups) heavy cream,
   whipped
Star anise, powdered, or if
   unobtainable, infuse 3-4 whole
   stars in a little of the cream by
   heating, then cooling, straining
   and whipping it

THE DECORATION
Ground hazelnuts or finely ground
   toasted almonds

Serves 8-10

STAR ANISE MAY not be peculiar to the region, but the local apéritif pastis certainly is, and in this dessert the one is brought in to enhance the other. The iced soufflé is a form of parfait, one of the few ice creams that can be made well without a churn. The method is a little tricky, but it can be quickly mastered, and the dessert may be made up to three days ahead.

Place the sugar and enough water to just cover it in a saucepan and bring to the boil. Over the heat, stir until the sugar dissolves; it must dissolve *before the water comes to the boil*. Boil the water down until the sugar reaches 118°C (244°F) on a sugar/deep fry thermometer. If not using a thermometer (and there's no need once you have got the feel), wait until it boils down to small, even-sized bubbles all the way across the top.
   Place the egg yolks in a large bowl. Pour on the syrup in a stream, as if making a mayonnaise, beating well. After incorporating the syrup, transfer the beater to a stand, if you have one, and beat until cool. This could take 15 minutes.
   When the syrup and egg-yolk mixture is cool, stir in the pastis. Fold in the cream, and enough powdered star anise to give the desired flavour.

Pour the mixture into a 1.2 L (1 qt) mould with an oiled, not buttered, collar of waxed paper. Leave a minimum of 6 hours in the freezer before serving. The added collar should allow the mixture to sit well above the true height of the mould. It is this that gives us the name *soufflé glacé*, although the mixture in any other format (e.g. moulded as a terrine) is technically a *parfait* (rich ice cream).

When ready to serve, peel off the paper, and either serve the soufflé as it is or, if you want to force the soufflé association, press some ground hazelnut or, better still, ground toasted almonds, onto the sides of the soufflé above the edge of the mould.

Iced soufflés and parfaits can be served on their own, or as an accompaniment to poached fruit. This one is excellent with poached peaches or pears.

LITTLE PILLOWS

Oreillettes

THE DOUGH
50 g (3 tablespoons) butter
250 g (2 cups) plain (all-purpose)
flour
2 eggs
30 mL (2 tablespoons) orange
flower water
30 mL (2 tablespoons) milk
25 g (2 tablespoons) sugar
Grated peel of 1 orange

2 L (2 qt) grape seed or peanut oil
for deep frying
Icing (confectioners') sugar

Serves 10-12

THESE 'LITTLE PILLOWS' are simply lengths of pastry dough deep-fried and dredged with icing (confectioners') sugar. Cut with a scallop-edged pastry cutter and twisted into pretty shapes, they are a favourite cookie for serving with champagne, as an afternoon tea break or when someone drops by for a visit.

The dough: Melt butter gently in a saucepan over a low heat, so that it does not change its flavour; set aside to cool. Place the flour in a food processor, add the melted butter, the eggs, orange water, milk, sugar and, lastly, the grated orange peel. Process until all the ingredients are well blended. Form into a ball, wrap in plastic wrap and rest about 2 hours in a cool place, or in the refrigerator in hot weather.

When ready, roll out the pastry to a thickness of 3 mm (⅛ in) and cut into strips of about 5 cm (2 in) width, then cut the strips into 2.5 cm (1 in) lengths. You now have rectangles 2.5 x 5 cm (1 x 2 in). Make two slits longitudinally in some of the rectangles, two side by side in others. Vary the shapes with some triangular pieces, and also make some triangles with a slit in the base through which you pull the tip of the triangle. Some people also pleat the dough into rough bow-like shapes.

To cook and serve the oreillettes: Fill a large saucepan or frying basket with enough depth of oil to deep-fry. Heat the oil to 180°C (350°F) and cook the *oreillettes,* a few at a time, until golden. Drain on paper towels and sprinkle with icing (confectioners') sugar. Serve warm or at room temperature. *Oreillettes* may be stored for a couple of days in an airtight tin, but are at their best when freshly made. May be served with fresh berries and/or raspberry coulis.

AIOLI

Aioli

3-6 large cloves garlic,
depending on strength
required
3 egg yolks
10 mL (2 teaspoons) Dijon-style
mustard
300-400 mL (1¼-1⅔ cups)
olive oil
Salt
White pepper
Vinegar or lemon juice

AIOLI, THE OLIVE OIL and garlic mayonnaise of Provence, was traditionally made in a mortar and pestle; where the cloves of garlic were pounded to a paste with just enough salt to add 'grip' to the pestle. Then the olive oil mayonnaise was made on top, directly in the mortar.

With an electric mixer, the method is quicker; with a food processor, even quicker, as the garlic can be ground with the blades, although it is not entirely crushed until the oil and egg mixture brings up the volume in the bowl.

If using a mixer, or hand-held whisk, break the eggs directly onto the puréed garlic, transferred to a small bowl. Beat the yolks a moment with the mustard, then add the oil drop by drop, taking care not to pour the oil too fast in the early stages, when the aioli is most likely to separate. As the egg starts to take the oil into emulsion, the oil may be poured faster, and providing you stir fast without allowing too much build up of oil, it may be poured in a steady stream until the aioli gets as thick as you wish to serve it.

The less oil, the richer the egg and garlic taste; more oil and the mixture is thicker.

140

Season with salt and pepper, and, if desired, add a little vinegar or lemon juice to taste, to bring up the acidity.

If using a food processor, roughly chop the garlic, place in the bowl and, using a pulse action, chop as finely as possible. Add the egg yolks and mustard (you may do better with 2 yolks and 1 whole egg), pulse again, then incorporate the oil by pouring slowly down the funnel. Season as above.

PISTOU

Pistou

3 cloves garlic
40 leaves fresh basil (don't even
try with dried)
Optional: 1 tomato, peeled and seeded
45 mL (3 tablespoons) olive oil
60 g (⅓ cup) grated Parmesan
cheese
Salt
Pepper

NAMED AFTER THE local dialect word for the pestle traditionally used to grind it, this garlic and basil paste is most famous in the thick vegetable *Soupe au Pistou* (page 51) where its pungent flavour enlivens what could well be a simple broth. *Pistou* is also wonderful on pasta, spread on pizza shells, with fish and lamb and even as a dressing for salads.

Today, the food processor does a good job. Process the garlic and basil until finely chopped, then add the tomato, if using. Pour the oil down the funnel and continue until the mixture becomes a paste, then add the Parmesan. Season with salt and pepper.

ROUILLE
Sauce Rouille

3 large cloves garlic, chopped
1 small or ½ larger red chilli
 (hot pepper), chopped
Few grains salt
3 egg yolks
400-500 mL (1½-2 cups) olive
 oil
Salt
Pepper
¼ teaspoon saffron threads

THIS 'RUST-COLOURED' SAUCE is the chilli and garlic mayonnaise traditionally served with the regional fish soups of southern France.

With a mortar and pestle, crush the garlic with the chilli. Use a few grains of salt to help hold the 'grip' of the pestle in the mortar. When it is well crushed, add the egg yolks, and, stirring well with a whisk, build an olive oil mayonnaise (as for the Aioli), on this base with the oil, seasoning with salt and pepper, but no vinegar. If the colour is not red enough to be called 'rouille' (rust-coloured), add a tiny pinch of saffron.

It is possible to do this in the base of a food processor, although the blades sometimes have trouble chopping this small quantity of garlic finely enough. Start by chopping the garlic and chilli finely, and if the garlic is caught beneath the blades and is not chopped at first, it should be done adequately so as the mayonnaise is built on the egg yolks.

ANCHOIADE
Anchoiade

500 mL (2 cups) olive oil (see
 note below)
150 g (5 oz) anchovy fillets,
 preferably salt-packed,
 washed, filleted and kept in
 olive oil.
 These are of finer quality
 than most canned ones, and
 less salty
3 cloves garlic, crushed
15 g (1 tablespoon) Dijon-style
 mustard
30 mL (2 tablespoons) wine
 vinegar

THIS RICHLY FLAVOURED ANCHOVY SAUCE is a Provençal favourite. It is most often served as a dip for crudités, but may also accompany beef dishes.

Put 150 mL (⅔ cup) olive oil in a saucepan with the filleted anchovies and cook slowly for 15 minutes. Remove from the heat. When cool, mash the anchovies into a paste and add the garlic, mustard and vinegar. You may do this with a hand whisk or in a food processor. Then add the remaining oil, blending slowly as for making a mayonnaise.

Note: The quantities above give a very liquid texture like a salad dressing. If using for crudités, reduce the oil to 250 mL (1 cup); the texture will be slightly more like that of a dip, and the sauce will adhere better to the vegetables.

TAPENADE

Tapénade

*250 g (½ lb) black olives (avoid
    the very salty ones), pitted
2 cloves garlic, crushed
80 g (2½ oz) anchovy fillets (see
    Anchoiade recipe)
80 g (2½ oz) capers
100 mL (1 scant cup) olive oil*

TAPENADE, LIKE *ANCHOIADE*, is an
anchovy-based paste rich in olive oil, but
unlike *anchioade*, the *tapénade* also contains
olives and capers. It may be spread on small
triangles of toast or bread to accompany the
apéritif, and is often used as a dip with
crudités. It may also appear as an
accompaniment to fish dishes or be spread
on rolled cuts of meat, most often beef or
lamb. Like many other Provençal sauces,
tapénade was originally made with a mortar
and pestle. Now the food processor and
blender have brought it into the realm of the
amateur cook.

Combine the olives with the garlic,
anchovies and capers in the bowl of a food
processor and reduce to a paste. Incorporate
the olive oil by pouring it slowly down the
funnel in a stream. You may choose to vary
the amount of oil to alter the thickness of
the *tapénade* according to the use to which it
will be put.

PISSALAT

Le Pissalat

*375 g (¾ lb) fresh sardines or
    mackerel, as small as possible
375 g (¾ lb) fresh anchovies (not dried or
    canned ones; if you cannot find fresh, use
    more sardines)
30 g (1½ tablespoons) rock salt
20 g (4 tablespoons) fresh
    ginger, peeled and grated
1 tablespoon mixed black and
    white peppercorns
3 small chillies, finely chopped
Pinch cinnamon and/or cloves*

PISSALAT WAS ORIGINALLY the fish paste
used as the base of the famous onion pizza
from Nice, the *Pissaladière*, this giving the
latter its name. Still made by traditional
cooks, the *Pissalat* is now rarely seen in
commercially baked *Pissaladière*, but it is
used as a fish spread for bread or croûtons,
and is a favourite at local picnics.

Remove the heads and bones of the fish. In a
small earthenware terrine, place a layer of
the fish, sprinkle with rock salt, ginger,
peppercorns and chillies. Repeat until you
have used up all the fish, finishing with a
layer of salt. Keep in a cool place (refrigerate
only in summer or in a hot climate) for 24
hours, then stir with a wooden spoon.
    Leave the mixture for one week, stirring
every night; and at the end of the week it
should have become a purée. Sieve (or use a
food processor) to make into a paste, then
place in a sealed jar covered with 60 mL
(4 tablespoons) olive oil. Although not a
preserve, it will last in the refrigerator for
2-3 weeks.

TOMATO SAUCE

Sauce Tomates

60 mL (4 tablespoons) olive oil
1 onion, diced or 1 tablespoon
finely chopped shallots
4 large tomatoes, peeled, seeded
and diced
2 cloves garlic, finely chopped
Sprig thyme or oregano (if using
basil it is shredded and added at
the last minute)
1 level teaspoon sugar
Salt
Pepper

AS SO MANY OF THE DISHES of Provence include a tomato sauce, it is useful to keep this recipe handy. Decide if you prefer the tomatoes cut through the sauce finely or roughly (the latter is sometimes known as *tomates concassées*). If a fine-textured sauce is needed, remove any sprigs or stalks of the herbs and pass through a sieve or mouli. The recipe may be lightened with a little cream, but this is strictly *not* Provençal.

Heat the oil in a pan and sauté the onion or shallots, depending on whether you want a stronger or finer sauce, and on the chunkiness desired, until softened. Add the tomatoes, garlic, chosen herb and sugar. Bring to the boil, reduce the heat and simmer gently for 20 minutes. Depending on desired chunkiness, mash with a spoon, then pass through a blender or food processor, or, for a fine sauce, pass through a sieve or mouli. Return to the saucepan, season and thin a little with water, if not to the desired consistency.

FRESH TOMATO COULIS

Coulis de Tomate

4-5 large ripe tomatoes, cored and
roughly chopped (peeled and
seeded before chopping if using
a food processor or blender)
15 mL (1 tablespoon) tomato paste
45 mL (3 tablespoons) olive oil
Salt
Pepper
1 teaspoon red or white wine vinegar
Optional: chopped parsley and/or
shredded basil

THOUGH THE TERM might translate as 'purée of fresh tomato', the word coulis in the English language means a sauce of fresh crushed fruit (for example, tomato, raspberry, strawberry, mango).

The best tomato coulis is pushed through a sieve or mouli to remove the seeds; if using a blender or food processor, peel and seed the tomatoes before starting. The tomatoes need not be peeled first if passed through a sieve or mouli, as the peel stays behind.

Warning: Fresh tomato coulis may be made in advance, but should be stored in a bowl, and stirred and spooned around the plates just before serving, as water will seep from the solids, spoiling the dish's appeal.

Using a sieve or mouli, combine the tomatoes and tomato paste and strain into a bowl. Whisk in the oil, salt, pepper and vinegar to taste. Finish with the herb(s), if desired.

In a food processor or blender, purée the tomato with the tomato paste, adding the oil and vinegar down the funnel. Season, and finish with the chosen herb(s).

INDEX